One Step Forward

The Life of Ken Dahlberg

I WAS THERE PRESS
Minneapolis, MN

One Step Forward

The Life of Ken Dahlberg

Al Zdon
Warren Mack

© 2008 Carefree Capital Inc.

ISBN-13 978-0-9799192-0-6
ISBN-10 0-9799192-0-7

Layout and design by Kendra Mack
Cover design by Kendra Mack

Printed in China by Petit Network, Inc.
Afton, MN

Distributed by Itasca Books Distribution
3501 Highway 100 South, Suite 220
Minneapolis, MN 55416
(952) 345-4488
(952) 920-0541 Fax
www.itascabooks.com

*Ken Dahlberg dedicates this book to his wife, BJ, and their family,
with special remembrance for his fallen comrades.*

The authors would like to thank:
Linda Mack for her writing assistance
Foster Friess and Dave Cavan for encouraging us to write this book
David Banks for his expert editing
Paul Waldon and Becky Arendt for their able assistance
Jo Anne Close and her colleagues at Fredrikson & Byron for transcribing interviews
Frank Olynyk, air-to-air combat historian
Dan Haulman and Patsy Robertson, Air Force Research Center
Bonnie Scheil for her help with the history of Miracle Ear
National Personnel Records Center, St. Louis, MO
National Military Archives, College Park, MD
American Fighter Aces Association
Nina Archabal, Director, Minnesota Historical Society
Bonnie Dunbar, President and CEO the Museum of Flight, Seattle, Washington
Martin and Barbara Dardis
The children of Denis and Madeleine Baudoin, Rosine, Sylvie, Dorothy, Cathy and Matthew
The members of the Dahlberg family, and especially Ken

Table of Contents

Dahlberg in front of a Ryan PT-22 Trainer after his first solo flight in King City, California.

Prologue

Capt. Ken Dahlberg was cruising at 10,000 feet in his P-47 Thunderbolt on February 14, 1945.

It had been a good day. Dahlberg, a twenty-seven-year-old Army Air Force pilot from St. Paul, Minnesota, had led a group of twelve aircraft on a successful dive bombing mission near Metz, Germany.

Dahlberg was one of his nation's top fighter pilots, accounting for fifteen kills, making him one of the rare triple aces in the war. He probably would have had more, but his squadron had been switched from flying the sleek P-51 Mustangs, hunting for German fighters, to flying missions in the sturdy P-47 Thunderbolt, dive bombing and strafing enemy positions. Plus, as the war went on, there were simply fewer German planes in the air.

World War II was winding down as the American and British forces were pushing into Germany from the west and the Russian Army was pressing towards Berlin on the east. Metz was an industrial center, and a frequent target of Allied bombing missions. It was well-protected by anti-aircraft guns, but the American squadron had made its run without incident.

It was Dahlberg's job to reassemble his group of P-47s and then head back to the base at Rosieres-en-Haye in France. All was going well.

Without warning, Dahlberg's aircraft took a direct hit from a German shell.

"The P-47 has protective armor behind the pilot, and that must be what saved me, because the airplane just blew up."

Knocked unconscious by the explosion and destruction of his plane, Dahlberg fell about 9,500 feet toward the earth. "I regained consciousness and pulled the rip cord at about 500 feet and had a very hard landing." His fellow pilots were certain that he was dead, the usual outcome of a direct hit by the large German artillery shell. "They said later all they saw were bits and pieces and no parachute. I must have been either a bit or a piece."

Twice before Dahlberg had been shot down behind enemy lines, and twice before he had escaped to fly again. This time, Dahlberg was miles from the American lines. His head was bleeding severely. He lost his compass and his escape kit.

There was only one thing to do, and it was what he always did when faced with a challenge. He headed off into the unknown.

The Dahlberg family in the summer of 1929, with parents Mamie and Harry in the back. The children, from left, are Ken, Harriet, Marcella, Harold, Arnie and Mervin.

Chapter One

Growing Up

Kenneth Harry Dahlberg grew up in the rolling hills and splendid farmland of western Wisconsin.

He once estimated that he milked 36,500 cows during his formative years. Well, not 36,500 cows exactly, but five cows, twice a day, 365 days a year for ten years. In fact, his birthday present one year was a new milk pail, and he was mighty happy to get it.

Dahlberg was born in 1917 in St. Paul, just fifty miles to the west across the border in Minnesota. "I was born the same year in America as communism was born in Russia," he said. "And I outlived it." His dad, Harry, was a motorman on St. Paul's streetcar line, and his route was from St. Paul to Stillwater, often taking families to the Wildwood amusement park at White Bear Lake.

Dahlberg claimed that at the age of one he talked his dad into moving to the farm. "I recall saying, 'Let's get out of here.' And my father said, 'Why?' And I said, 'I think Minnesota is going to be a socialist state.' And my father said, 'Well, when people escape, they usually go to the closest border.' And so my father, in his wisdom, took my mother and my older brother and me over the border to a little hardscrabble farm" near Wilson, Wisconsin, a town of about 200 where Harry Dahlberg had been raised.

Dahlberg's mother, Mamie, had grown up in Minneapolis and was of Norwegian descent. "My mother had an eighth-grade education, and she had a big talent. She could really play the piano. She told my father we could move to the country if she could take her upright piano. She would play the piano all the time in that little house in Wilson."

Mamie Dahlberg, Ken's mother.

When the family moved back to Wilson in 1918, the senior Dahlberg converted his motorcar earnings into a 40-acre farm with a log barn. When Ken was seven years old, the family moved to a 120-acre farm that cost his father $6,000.

During the Depression, the family lost the farm when the Federal Land Bank foreclosed on the land. "It wasn't only because there was a Great Depression, but there was a seven-year dry spell. I remember my father saying that he could handle the Depression, but he couldn't handle the drought."

When the rains returned, the family repurchased the farm for $3,000. "My father had to put $600 down to get the farm back, and I don't know how he did that. There just wasn't a lot of currency floating around in those days."

After that, the family began to function a little more normally. By then, normal meant ten people at the dinner table: mother and father, six kids, and two grandparents.

"I'm not saying we were poor, but when Mom threw the dog a bone, he had to signal for a fair catch. You ate what you killed or grew. Milk was our main cash crop. We sold milk to the local cheese factory, and we would get a check for nine dollars for two weeks' worth of milk. We would also bring our eggs to the local grocer and trade them for our staples — flour, sugar, salt and pepper, and other things. There were no days off on the farm. I would try to supplement our table with a squirrel or rabbit, and it was expected that I would expend one .22-caliber short bullet for every animal I brought home. I would try to shoot them in the head, and then I could skin them out. In the Sears Roebuck catalog, you could get what was called a stretcher. You put the rawhide skin on it, and you dried it. You could get twenty-five cents for each hide down at the grocery store. So we ate the meat and sold the hides."

Another source of income came in the fall with the harvest of a neighbor's butternut trees. "We would get permission to pick the butternuts, and then we would put them up on our roof to dry. After a couple of months they would dry out, and we'd crack them with a hammer. For a quart, you could get twenty-five cents from the grocer. We were just trying to find ways to make a buck.

"The good thing about all this was that we didn't have newspapers, radio or television, so we didn't have Walter Cronkite to tell us we were poor. We just didn't know. We just got on with life."

Clothing was almost always secondhand, except for the new overalls that every child got in the fall for school. Dahlberg had an aunt in St. Paul who would give the family cast-off clothing. "My mother wore men's shoes. It really didn't matter much in the country. She wasn't going anywhere."

Dahlberg's parents both had a spiritual side, but not quite in the same way. "We got our basic understanding, and stories like the three wise men and the birth of Christ from my mother. But Father had this responsibility of feeding all these mouths in the middle of the Depression, and so he had a different take on it. He felt that God helps those who help themselves, and we grew up with that."

The farmhouse had three bedrooms. The parents' bedroom was downstairs. The girls had one bedroom upstairs, and the boys had the other. "We didn't need any furnishings or place to hang your clothes, because there weren't any clothes to hang. You just didn't have any. What you didn't have on your back was in the wash. As for shoes, you had whatever you wore. Mother had to wash all that barnyard dirt, and she had to do all that on a scrub board. Later on, we got a

Ken (on right) and older brother, Mervin, circa 1920.

little Maytag washing machine. We didn't have any electricity, but the machine had a little putt-putt engine on it. That was the greatest piece of equipment we ever acquired on the farm. We also had a little engine in the well house to bring up the water. You'd still have to carry it into the house. On Saturday night, we'd all take baths, and we'd fight over who got the first bath, because that was the cleanest water."

Ken, Harriet and Arnie visiting the family farm, summer 2006.

Around the table, it was sometimes bedlam. "There was such a range of ages there. Everything was cooked on a wood stove, and everywhere in the house was lit by kerosene. We all ate at 5 p.m. so that dad could get to the barn by 6. Life was simple. For my eighth birthday, I got a new milk pail. That was a big deal for me. It was the shiniest pail in the barn."

The water in the well house was very cold, and once the milking was done, the milk would be poured into a big can and placed in the cold water, ready for the milkman to pick it up the next morning and take it to the cheese factory. "We had a separator, and we made our own butter. One day at church we saw an ice-cream maker. We had never seen one before and, boy, that was something. We finally got an ice-cream maker. No wonder I have clogged arteries."

Mamie would bake something everyday, and twice a week she would bake bread for the household. "In the end she would take little dabs of bread dough and put a little sugar or honey on it, something to sweeten it up, and they came out just like Dunkin' Donuts."

The bathroom was, of course, outdoors. "We had a two-holer. In the winter you kind of got in and got out in a hurry. We had ten people using this little two-holer, guys and girls the same. You had to take turns. But nobody thought anything of it. I don't remember it being a problem. And everybody used the catalog hanging from the wall. Later in life, in my business, in my marketing business, I wound up with Sears Roebuck being one of my strategic partners. That's the bookend to that story."

The family attended church at a tiny Methodist church in Wilson. Ministers came only now and then. When it was time for a Dahlberg to get confirmed, the family traveled about three miles south of town, to the Lutheran church. "I grew up as a Lutheran. In those days, when people grew up in a religion, they would stay with it."

Wilson had two mercantile stores, a small bank, a department store and two saloons. The stores had most of the staples of life, like food and socks. "But in the fall we would go to the closest shopping hub, in Menomonie. It was probably fifteen miles away. We'd get a new pair of overalls and a new pair of shoes for school."

The trips to town were by horse when Dahlberg was very young, but his father bought a 1917 Model-T Ford in 1922. Still, because the roads were impassable in the winter and spring, horse power was still the way to go much of the year.

One of the community's major amenities was a schoolhouse. "There were four of us in my class, and about thirty or thir-

Main Street in Wilson, Wisconsin, February 2007.

ty-five in the whole school. My father was clerk of the school board, and he would buy four books each fall for each class. The books weren't for the students, but for the teacher."

Two of the kids in Dahlberg's class were twins who lived on a farm about three miles away. Esther and Virgil Sorenson rode a horse to school everyday, and there was a small horse barn on the school grounds.

"This was obviously before the days of running water, and, as far as the Sorenson twins were concerned, before the days of soap. Virgil's nickname was Porky, for obvious reasons. We would often play marbles at lunch time, since there weren't any gymnasiums or auditoriums. I was a little better than Porky, and it came to pass that I won all of Porky's marbles. He wanted them back really bad, and he said he'd trade a piglet for the marbles. I had more marbles than I needed, I guess. At least I had more marbles than I did piglets, and I told him it was a deal. He brought this little squealer to school one day in a burlap sack, and I carried him home — about a mile to our house.

"My father said, 'Where'd you get the piglet?' He thought I'd stolen it. I told him the story. Not long after that, my father ran into Porky's father, probably at the post office. He said, 'Did you know that Porky gave my boy a pig?' His father said he didn't know that. Later, my father told me I was obliged — well, he didn't say it that way — to bring the pig back to Porky. And I said, 'Why? I won it fair and square. It's my pig.' My father said Porky didn't have permission to trade the pig from his father, and that he'd swiped it. I said,

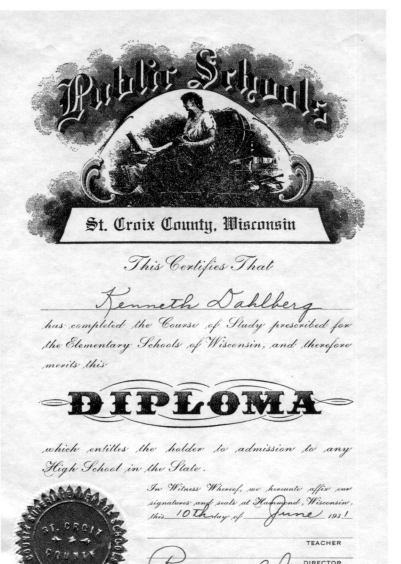

'Well, I don't know about that. All I know is that I won it fair and square.' My father responded, 'Well, sometimes we've got to pay for other people's mistakes, and we must do it graciously.' I didn't know what incredible advice he was giving me.

"I brought the pig back, but I've been a glutton for ham and bacon ever since — trying to make up for it."

A big outing for the Dahlberg family, once they had their Model T, was to cross the state line and visit their relatives in Minnesota. "We had an aunt and uncle in Mahtomedi, and we thought they were our rich relatives. He was a janitor for Mahtomedi High School, and his wife, my aunt, cooked for one of the swells. That's what we called wealthy people. We thought our relatives were rich because they had a new car, and a nice house and stuff, and they lived in the city. They would take us down to the lake, and we would go swimming. It was a big deal for us."

Dahlberg's first job off the farm as a teenager was shoveling sand into a wagon for a road crew. It was part of a Depression-era Works Progress Administration program. He was paid ten cents an hour, and he worked ten hours a day.

"I got to talking with the guy who had the wagon, and I found out he was paid fifteen cents an hour for his two horses and wagon, plus he got the same ten cents I was getting. So he was getting twenty-five cents an hour. I found out who the boss was, and I was able to use my family's team of horses one day a week. So, on one day of my workweek, I was making twenty-five cents an hour. I was getting some collateral value out of our horses. I was employing capital — my father's capital. Two horsepower capital. That was my first paycheck, and I got it from the government." "At least I was doing dsomething useful," said Dahlberg, "I was building roads."

When Dahlberg got to his senior year, it was decided that he would go live with his aunt and attend an accredited high school, St. Paul Harding. "I went from a class of four to a class of about 400."

Dahlberg's uncle, Harry Zimmerman, was a vice president of International Harvester in Moline, Ill., in charge of the company's foreign operations. Earlier, he had been sent by the company to Germany, where he had built ten large International Harvester plants. In 1935, he saw the war clouds forming, and sent his wife, Anna, and two children back to St. Paul while he stayed in Germany. "I had to go someplace to finish my high school, and this was the logical thing to do. Because she was without a man in the house, it was my job to stoke the coal furnace. I learned all about that stuff. I also did other chores around the house, whatever guys are supposed to do."

Harding High School was a revelation after the two-room schoolhouse of his previous eleven years of public education. "My first observation when I saw that big basketball court was that it would sure hold a lot of hay. It was ten times as big as our hay mow. Plus they had all these playing fields and different sports, and in the high school building there were so many rooms. The biggest problem was finding out which room to go to next, and remembering the next teacher's name. It was a culture shock."

Dahlberg was trying to fit into a high-school culture that had been developing for four years for the seniors. He went to class like everyone else, and he went to lunch like everyone else, and he walked to school like everyone else, but the connection to his classmates was fragile.

"I was out of the conversation. They would talk about sports, and I wouldn't know what they're talking about. They'd talk about school, and I wouldn't know what they're talking about. It's like being excluded, and the feeling of inferiority overwhelms you some-

Ken on the day of his confirmation, October 18, 1931.

times. It's like you just can't hear or something. And I never got into sports because I didn't have any background. The only sport I was any good at, they didn't have in their program — marbles.

"Academically I did just fine. I think I was a B student, and the academics didn't seem too hard. It was the social integration that was lacking. But you know what? I was not uncomfortable. I just didn't know any differently. You only know what you know."

Ken poses with his friends Norm and Dick Schaefer on the bumper of his new Ford convertible in South Bend, Indiana, in 1938. "It was owned by me and the bank."

Chapter Two

The Hotel Business

Dahlberg graduated with the class of 1935, and his first job was at the Lowry Hotel in downtown St. Paul. "I didn't want to go back to the farm. I was ready to set out, but it was the Depression, and there were still four kids at home. It was necessary to get some money. In those days there just wasn't any money."

The Lowry and the St. Paul Hotel were considered the finest hostelries in the city. Dahlberg started at the absolute bottom rung, washing pots and pans in the Lowry's kitchen. The workweeks were sometimes seven days, and he often worked twelve hours in a day. Much of the work was at night after the meals had been cooked. When his day was done, Dahlberg would head back to his room at the YMCA in downtown St. Paul.

"Farm kids were used to working early, working late — they had a lot of energy. It was part of our in-grained culture.

"My first promotion was the most significant promotion in my whole life. I got promoted to dishwasher. If you've ever washed pots and pans in a hotel, anything is a promotion."

Dahlberg got to know the hotel's chef, René Boursier, one of the best chefs in the Twin Cities. Boursier took a liking to the young lad and moved him from the kitchen into the restaurant as a busboy. Boursier later opened his own restaurant in St. Paul, called René's, and it was considered the epitome of French restaurants in the capital city.

The Hotel Oliver, South Bend, Indiana.

Dahlberg's next job at the hotel was in the receiving department. He worked closely with the chef on what to expect each day. "It's important in the food business, particularly in the upscale food business, that you have someone who's very careful in the receiving area. I grew up on the farm, and I knew produce and I knew meat. I would have to look at the lettuce to make sure it didn't have any rust on it. I would have to make sure that people were selling us fresh vegetables. I'd have to check the meat to see how it was aged. You could only know these things from experience. And, of course, if you're working in receiving, you also get to do some accounting. The hotel had several restaurants and bars, and so it was a big business. And that led me into the accounting department."

The Lowry Hotel at that time had hired an outside accounting firm called Horwath and Horwath, a company that specialized in hotel accounting. The company placed a resident auditor at the larger hotels. At the smaller properties, it would share an employee with the hotel. Dahlberg, over time, developed a connection with the Horwath firm and eventually he got a job as food and beverage controller with the Antlers Hotel in Indianapolis. The Pick chain that owned the Antlers was one of the largest in the United States, with twenty-three hotels. Dahlberg worked for Horwath and Horwath, but he was on the hotel's payroll. From there he transferred to the Fort Meigs Hotel in Toledo, then to the Mark Twain Hotel in St. Louis. His job was to set up an accounting and control system at these hotels for their food and beverage systems.

The Mark Twain was a historic old hotel by the waterfront, but it had a tired, seldom-frequented coffee shop. "The head Pick guy for food and beverage was Edgar Moss, and he was in Chicago. We had many discussions about this coffee shop. It was my job to put some life into it. I told the Pick guy that I had a lot of experience eating out. Actually, the only place I ate out at was the White Castle, but I liked the way at the White Castles where you could see the guy that's cooking, and he had on a nice white chef's hat, and everything looked clean and inviting. So we agreed that we'd have an open kitchen."

The newly designed coffee shop had to have a name. "We were going to serve mainly hamburgers, and I was thinking about a name with 'cow' in it. I remembered a poem I knew in school."

I never saw a Purple Cow,
I never hope to see one;
But I can tell you, anyhow,
I'd rather see than be one.
— Gelett Burgess

"We just decided to call it the Purple Cow. It was such a success that by the time I got drafted, they had three or four Purple Cows going in the Pick hotels."

A want ad written by Ken.

Dahlberg was so delighted with the success of the Purple Cows that he talked with Moss about expanding the concept. "I told Moss that people like these things. We could have these all over the place. I didn't have a clue at the time what a chain was. But Moss said no, that we were in the hotel business, not the restaurant business. In today's world it would have been an incredibly good concept. It could have preempted the Golden Arches."

The next stop on the hotel trail for Dahlberg was the Hotel Oliver in South Bend, Indiana, the home of the University of Notre Dame. It was also the home city of the Studebaker auto company, and the Hotel Oliver was a key meeting and eating place for both organizations. Dahlberg was still working for Horwath, and his duties included running the food and beverage part of the Oliver, considered the jewel of the Pick chain. As such, he was in charge of hiring young hotel professionals from the college ranks, even though his own degree was from Harding High School.

"I learned that Cornell was the leading provider. If you could get somebody out of Cornell, you really had a coup. I started hiring these young people out of Cornell, and I thought they were really dumb. They didn't know anything. I had grown up in this world — I had grown up from the very seeds and the very calves of the plant and animal kingdom that we ate. Then I saw the application and the mass application of it in the big city. I found out these kids could add and subtract really fast, but they didn't know what they were adding. But it was a good situation for both of us, because we get our experience by association."

Though he worked for Horwath, Dahlberg did many other tasks at the Oliver. "My loyalty had to be with

Ken and family with Ken's new 1941 Ford convertible. From left: Harry, Mervin, Harriet, Harold, Mamie, Ken, Marcella, Arnie.

Horwath and Horwath, and that was understood between the accounting firm and the hotel. That was where my responsibility was. But just like on the farm, you don't just do one job, you do a thousand jobs."

And so, each night after a full day's work in accounting, Dahlberg would don his tuxedo and become the maitre d' in the main dining room at the Oliver. It was the first formal dining room he had worked at, and every night he would rub shoulders with the Studebakers, the Notre Dame elite, and the others who came to dine at the finest place in town.

One of those movers and shakers was the president of Notre Dame, the Rev. John Francis O'Hara, who convinced Dahlberg that he should enroll. Dahlberg started by taking two courses the first quarter, but had to lighten that load to one course. Even then, it was a struggle to balance his professional duties and new-found academic career. "One night I was standing at the food checker's desk, because that was part of the maitre d's job to check everything on the tray and make sure it matches what is on the check before it goes into the dining room. I was standing there, but my head was buried in a textbook. The manager of the Oliver was in the dining room that night, entertaining some important guests, and he was getting bad service. He walked into the kitchen to find out where the maitre d' was, and he saw me standing there, not even looking up from my book. He wasn't happy. He grabbed the book and said, 'You get back to where you belong, because at this hour you are on my payroll.' That was the end of my academic career. I just couldn't do both. I told the president at Notre Dame, and he sympathized. He always said I'd be back someday."

When Warner Brothers came to South Bend to make the movie "Knute Rockne, All American," starring Pat O'Brien and Ronald Reagan, Dahlberg got a chance to be an extra. Later he got a check from Jack Warner, the head of the studio, for $25. "Now, I don't know if he gave me that check for being in his movie, or whether it was a parting gift because I kind of took care of him in the dining room at the Oliver. For many years I had a copy of that check."

Dahlberg later had another encounter with his boss that was one of the major crises in his young career. The hotel manager would often entertain the important people from South Bend in his rooms, and often at the end of these luncheons or breakfasts, a collection would be taken up for the meal and a tip for the waiters. Dahlberg had attended one of these functions, and the next Monday morning he was hard at work at his calculator, toting up the food business that had gone on in the hotel that weekend. When

Ken in another of his sporty cars in Moline, Illinois.

he came to the manager's event, he was surprised to find that the money collected for the meal wasn't accounted for. "I saw this check for a dozen people or so at the manager's apartment, and he had charged the whole thing off to the entertainment account and had pocketed the money he collected."

The situation created a dilemma for Dahlberg. "I'm responsible for the auditing, but do I tell on my boss? Well, where I came from, you knew who you were responsible to, and I was responsible to Horwath. I called my mentor, a guy named Tom Knapp, and I told him what had happened. He said, "Holy shit, the manager did that?' I asked him what I was supposed to do. He told me it had to be reported, and, of course, this was very bad news for my boss. He almost lost his job. I told my boss at Horwath, though, that I was sure this was just an oversight on the manager's part. They knew I was being kind, but this was what you had to do in that kind of delicate situation. It was the first lesson I had in diplomacy."

The incident went right to the top, and Albert Pick Jr. became involved. "My name became known throughout the Pick organization at that point, and the whole event was used as a corporate lesson. I had saved the manager's job by saying it was an oversight, but the message was clear: Be careful of your oversights."

Dahlberg had one other experience with the Pick family, one that almost made him a member of the family. "When I was still at the Toledo Hotel, I had bought a new car, and I had to go to Chicago to report to corporate headquarters. Well, Mrs. Pick, the wife of the owner, said, 'If you don't mind, I'd love to ride back with you,' and she did. She talked about her daughter on the ride, and she was assuming the role of a matchmaker. So I got to date the boss's daughter. We had a couple of lunches, but I still had a girlfriend in St. Louis, not too serious but a little serious. Her name was Theresa Bussman. Her father had invented the Buss fuse that you see all over the world." Neither the Bussman nor the Pick romance worked out for Dahlberg, but another match made in heaven was on the horizon: The U.S. Army.

Ken as an Army Air Force cadet.

Chapter Three

Army Training

Dahlberg was twenty-three years old when he got his first induction notice. Because this was before the United States entered World War II, there was often a considerable amount of time between the first notice and the actual induction. In Dahlberg's case, it was almost a year.

As the months ticked away, Dahlberg anticipated that the call could come at any point. He quit his job with Pick and traveled around for a couple of months, coming home to Wisconsin and Minnesota. In late 1941, he got his notice to report to Fort Leonard Wood in Missouri for boot camp. He was officially inducted into the United States Army on November 2, 1941. It was a month before the Japanese bombed Pearl Harbor and pushed America into the war.

After his six weeks of basic training, he was given orders to the coast artillery at Fort Eustis in Virginia. One morning at Fort Eustis, Dahlberg and his peers were assembled when the corporal in charge asked for a volunteer to take one step forward.

"We were standing at attention, and we were very uncomfortable in our ill-fitting uniforms. We were making twenty-one dollars a month. Being unsatisfied where I was at, I took one step forward."

The corporal barked out again, "Men, look at Private Dahlberg. He's a leader. He's one step ahead of all of you."

Looking back, Dahlberg said, "I learned a lesson from a thirty-dollar-a-month professor. It was a step into

Ken was assigned to the coast artillery at Fort Eustis, Virginia. It was here that he applied to be an aviation cadet.

the unknown, a response to curiosity, a response to be more confident. It was one of the great lessons in my life."

It was also a long weekend doing KP at the mess hall, but the determination to take that step forward never faded from Dahlberg's outlook on life. Not long afterward, he saw a posting for cooks-and-bakers school. "It was the only thing that seemed logical, because I had the background. Plus, I figured I'd be the first one at the trough every day."

Dahlberg earned his graduation from the school. In the process of attending, he had to be present in the headquarters building, and it was there that he saw a posting on the bulletin board for two aviation cadets.

"To qualify for those two openings, you had to either have two years of college, or you had to take an equivalency test. I didn't have the college, so I took the test, and I must have done all right, because I got my name in the hat. After that they told me I needed two letters of recommendation. I scratched my head trying to think of two people who would do that. Then it came to me. I wrote to the mayor of South Bend, Jesse Pavey, and also to Notre Dame's previous football coach, Elmer Layden. Layden was commissioner of the National Football League by this time. I knew them both from my days at the Oliver Hotel. They both sent letters of recommendation, but sometimes you just have to have a little luck. The guy who was interviewing me was a graduate of guess where? Yes, Notre Dame. That's where the luck comes in."

Dahlberg had to wait for the slots to open up, and when they did he was sent across the country to Santa Ana, California, for the first phase of cadet training, called ground school. The course lasted for six months, and it was taught through the Army's military academy at West Point. "I remember they told me when I got there that there won't be any of the liberal arts. It will all be hard sciences and math, and it will all be a cram course. It will all be West Point style. Your demeanor was important, because you not only had to know all of the ground school requirements of becoming a pilot, you were also transitioning into becoming an officer. You won't become an officer until you get your wings, and you won't get your wings unless your deportment has been consistent with being an officer during your flight training. That was the mantra."

After ground school, there were three phases of further flight training, called primary, basic and advanced. For primary, Dahlberg was sent to King City, California, where he got his first flight experience on the Ryan PT-22. The Ryan Aeronautical Company had earned its reputation from building Charles Lindbergh's Spirit of St. Louis, but the PT-22 was somewhat

THE NATIONAL FOOTBALL LEAGUE

BROOKLYN, N. Y.
CHICAGO (BEARS) ILL.
CHICAGO (CARDINALS)
CLEVELAND, OHIO
DETROIT, MICH.

GREEN BAY, WIS.
NEW YORK, N. Y.
PHILADELPHIA, PA.
PITTSBURGH, PA.
WASHINGTON, D. C.

January 30, 1942

310 SOUTH MICHIGAN AVENUE
CHICAGO, ILLINOIS

Pvt. Kenneth H. Dahlberg
Battery 'B' 4th Battalion
Fort Eustis, Virginia

Dear Ken:

      Enclosed please find the letter of recommendation you requested. I do hope you are most successful in obtaining your desire to be a Flying Cadet.

      Hope everything is going nicely with you, and with sincere personal regards, I am

      Yours cordially,

Encl.
HTN

Elmer F. Layden,
Commissioner

ANS-APR 25th

Cover letter for the letter of recommendation from Elmer Layden, former Notre Dame football coach and NFL commissioner.

underpowered. "It had such a small engine that we called it the 'Maytag Messerschmitt.' Many of us farm kids had their first exposure to machinery with those putt-putt Maytag washing machines."

Primary was not easy for Dahlberg. "It did not come naturally to me. As a matter of fact, at the end of eight hours of flying, my instructor turned me over to another instructor for a second opinion. My instructor would not let me solo. I was in real danger of being washed out, and that's the biggest disappointment. It's worse than being shot, because then you went to bombardier school or something and you didn't get to be a pilot.

"I was to have one more chance, and they called it the washout flight. When I was coming in for a landing, I did a snap roll. It wasn't a slow roll at all. I snapped that roll big time. After we landed, the instructor said, 'What in the world got into you to do that maneuver?' And I said, 'Sir, I realized that this could be my last flight in a military plane, and I wanted to get the absolute most out of it.' And he said, 'You just passed.'

Dahlberg got to solo, and moved on to basic flight training at Chico, California, where the aircraft had bigger engines — much bigger. From the 130-horsepower primary trainer, the new fliers now were in command of a Vultee BT-13 with a 450-horsepower radial engine. "It shook like the dickens. We called it the Vultee Vibrator. But, as any pilot can tell you, the exhilaration of power is addictive. The pedal to the metal. It's just like your car — you want a little more horsepower. They climb faster, they maneuver better, and it makes you feel better."

Dahlberg also did basic instrument training in the BT-13. Part of that training was listening to two radio signals using the Morse code letters A and N. The pilot would correct the direction of the aircraft until the two signals were united, or the pilot was in the "cone" or on a solid beam. It was called "flying the beam," and if either the dit-dot or the dot-dits got louder in the radio headset, the pilot would need to correct his course. The pilot also had to consider the wind, making the whole problem very difficult at times.

After fifty more hours of instruction, the survivors of Dahlberg's class moved on to advanced training at Luke Field near Phoenix, Arizona. It was at this point that the sheep and goats were separated. Some pilots went on to train in fighters, while others were assigned to bombers. Nearly all the young trainees wanted the glamour and speed of the fighters, and only a few were interested in the more pedestrian chore of delivering payloads to distant targets. Dahlberg was chosen to fly fighters.

"I suppose they were profiling you right from the beginning. They never did publish what the criteria were, and I don't think they wanted to publish that. I know that later on, when I was an instructor, you just knew instinctively which way a pilot should go."

One of the first officers Dahlberg ran into at Luke Field was a young ground-school instructor named Barry Goldwater, who was a native of Phoenix. Goldwater had been a civilian pilot and had ferried planes in the military, but he was not a military flier. His family owned one of the leading department stores in the Southwest.

"We became friends because one of the courses that he taught in advanced training was skeet shooting. The reason they taught skeet was because the city kids had never had a gun in their hand, and they didn't have a clue on how to lead a target. If you grow up with something, you have a great advantage. Farm kids grew up with a gun in their hands, and we only ate what we could kill. One day Barry said to me, 'I wish I had an easier way, a faster way to explain this,'" and I told him I had an idea. We hooked a water hose to the skeet gun, and as you're moving the hose, the water is trailing it. So you've got to get out and keep out in front of it. If you want to hit something, you've got to keep moving. You can't stop. The water hose became part of the training manual, and Barry and I became pretty good friends."

Graduation from Luke Field when Ken received his wings and was commissioned an officer, 1942.

The aircraft for the trainees at Luke Field was the biggest one yet. The AT-6, built by North American, had a 550-horsepower radial engine. It was also the first aircraft the trainees flew that was equipped with guns, a .30-caliber in each wing.

"We would go down to the gunnery range down by Ajo, Arizona, near the border. We would practice strafing the ground targets, and we'd also practice aerial gunnery. An AT-6 would be towing a target, and there would be four ships in a formation. They would dip the tips of the bullets for each plane in a

different color. You didn't know how many hits you got until they dropped the target, and you could go look at it.

"We also learned more instrument flying, and we had to learn about lowering the landing gear. One day a cadet landed with his wheels up. When we asked how he missed the tower screaming at him to lower the gear, he said the gear warning horn was so loud he couldn't hear anything."

The trainees did some rudimentary attack tactics on the target, and learned that a thirty-degree attack angle was the optimum. They learned

Ken trained other pilots in the AT-6 at Yuma in April, 1943. This trainer was what he was flying when he decided to go under some power cables over the Colorado River.

loops and slow rolls and snap rolls, and what the pilots considered the ultimate combat techniques (such as the chandelle — a steep climbing turn), aerobatics that were developed by fighter pilots in World War I. Many of these maneuvers pushed the airplane to its maximum. "In combat, it often becomes a matter of who's going to stall out first."

As graduation neared, the Army reserved the right to make one final selection, and some of the pilots were sent off to bomber school. Pilots didn't know for sure which direction they would be heading until they got their orders. Dahlberg graduated from advanced training with Class 42-K on December 3, 1942, got his wings, and was commissioned a second lieutenant. His first assignment was to be an instructor at a new airfield in Yuma, Arizona. It would be fighter training.

With the Air Corps growing quickly, the Army had to take some of its better new fliers and put them right back into the program as trainers.

"I was going over to Yuma on the train, and, guess what, there sat Barry Goldwater. He had just been promoted from being a ground-school instructor at Luke to heading up the new base ground school at Yuma. So now, as buddies we get to Yuma, and all they've got is an airstrip with some airplanes and a bunch of tents. Barry and I took a tent together, and we lived in that tent for about five months.

"Barry said he knew the owner of the El Cortez Hotel in Yuma, and at least we'll have a good place to stay on the weekends. So we commandeered a Jeep and headed down there, but some tank division that was practicing in the desert had commandeered the entire hotel for themselves. The owner found us a little closet, and we took some folding tents and strung them up with string or wire, and put one above the other. Barry told me I was younger and had to take the top one. And that was how we slept in the famous El Cortez Hotel."

While at Yuma, Dahlberg was able to give Goldwater some clandestine training in a primary trainer assigned to the base. Later Goldwater went on to earn his wings and ended his career in the Air Force as a general.

Dahlberg's job was to train advanced cadets. "One of the toughest decisions I've ever had to make in my life was whether or not to wash out a cadet. But then you think this guy might kill himself, so maybe you're saving his life. But we knew how much passion these cadets had because we knew how much we didn't want to wash out ourselves."

It was at Yuma that Dahlberg did what he calls one of the dumbest things in his military career. "I noticed that one of the cadets seemed to be hesitant about the dive bombing. He just didn't like to get that close to the ground. I said, 'You've got to get it down there.' So I took the stick and rolled it over and showed him the typical bombing run. While I was down there, I had this little temptation to do a little buzzing, because we were right by the Colorado River. I was having fun buzzing the Colorado River from the backseat, when all of a sudden there were a whole bunch of big wires coming up fast in front of me. I was too low to get over them, so I decided to go under them.

"When you put the stick down, the initial reaction of the airplane isn't to go down, but to simply point down. It was at that precise moment that the plane scraped the high-tension wires. There was a big, blinding flash, a fire flash. The wires took off the antenna, they took off the canopy, and they took off the tail, the vertical tail. Cut them right off.

"The cadet was slumped over in the front seat, and I was sure he was dead. But now I was wondering how I was ever going to get this thing back to the base."

The cadet regained consciousness on the way back, and somehow Dahlberg managed to bulldog the damaged AT-6 back to the base at Yuma. It was at that point that he found that he had clipped the wires that brought power from the Hoover Dam to the city, and all of Yuma was without power.

"I knew my military career was over at that point. You just can't do things like that. But this was where I learned my first lesson in leverage. I had an IOU in my pocket for nine hundred dollars from the commanding officer of the base. He was addicted to gambling, and the night before we'd been playing poker, and then that had led to craps. When I was called in to see him, I just took the IOU out of my wallet and I put it on his desk and said, 'Well, I guess I won't be needing this anymore.' I also told him that I'd be willing to take any kind of duty if I could keep my job."

P-40s in formation during the training of Chinese officers at Luke Field, Arizona.

The commanding officer was lenient with Dahlberg, allowing him to keep flying, but confining him to base for thirty days. He also assigned him the job of being in charge of the base's prison compound.

"I said, 'Thank you, sir,' and I got in the Jeep and went over to the stockade. The first thing I saw were a half-dozen big, husky prisoners behind the stockade, and I got really scared. But the second thing I saw were a couple of Indian motorcyles. I had always wanted to ride a motorcycle, and here were two of them assigned to the stockade. They were both mine. Not only that, but they had red lights on them, and a siren."

Dahlberg couldn't leave the base, but he amused himself by riding around it, using his lights and siren, and pulling his fellow instructors over to give them warning tickets.

Toward the end of the month, there was a crash at the end of the runway. "I raced out there on my motorcycle to check it out. I forgot to slow down, and I hit the sand at about seventy miles an hour. They took me to the hospital. I think there was sand in every opening in my body."

The base commander came to see Dahlberg at the hospital. "He took one look at me and said, 'I'm going to cut you orders for combat before you kill yourself in training.' And that's how I got out of Yuma, but I was sad because I lost my motorcycle."

Dahlberg's next orders were not for Europe, however. Instead, he was sent back to Luke Field in Phoenix to lead more advanced training. This time the plane was the P-40, and it was Dahlberg's job to train a group of Chinese officers as part of a combat training unit. It was the first time that actual combat aircraft were used in training.

Neither the instructor nor the Chinese pilots knew each other's language, which made training difficult at times. "The first thing you had to do was get them soloed on that airplane, and I was standing on the wing giving this guy last-minute instructions when he hit the throttle. The prop wash blew me off the plane and onto the runway, and I broke my wrist. At least I got to go home for ten days."

Dahlberg enjoyed the Chinese pilots, but sometimes their ability to fly was in question. "For some reason, they didn't get it right

A group of Chinese trainees, Luke Field, Arizona. Ken is fourth from the right in the front row.

away. They had lots of accidents. I wondered if it was because of how they were chosen to be in the pilot program, not based on their skills, but on whose kid they were. One of my students was the son of Claire Chennault, the leader of the Flying Tigers, and his Chinese wife, Ann. Plus they were coming from a different culture. It wasn't a power or machinery-based culture."

While at Luke, Dahlberg had another chance to step forward for an assignment. "Somebody asked for volunteers to fly a General McMahon from Luke over to Palm Springs, and, of course, I volunteered. I flew him over to his meeting, and afterwards I flew him back in the AT-6. My fellow pilot had Colonel D.C. McNair on board. Later on, it came down through channels that there was severe criticism of my takeoff at Palm Springs. They said I did a chandelle at takeoff. I was momentarily in very serious trouble because it was official word from the tower, and how can you deny that? So I decided I'd take a chance on General McMahon, and he wrote back that not only had the pilot not done a chandelle, but 'I want to compliment the pilot on his superb flight skills.' I still have a copy of that letter. Later on, Colonel McNair became a

ARMY AIR FORCES PILOT SCHOOL
(ADVANCED-SINGLE ENGINE)
Luke Field, Phoenix, Arizona

7 September 1943

S T A T E M E N T

I led a formation of two (2) AT-6's off the Palm Springs Field
at approximately 1730 on August 29, 1943, enroute to Luke Field
via Hyder, Arizona. General J. B. McMahon of the 77th Division was
passenger in my plane and Colonel D. C. McNair was passenger in Lieutenant
Kelley's plane. On take off, I made a moderately steep turn in order
to get out of the prop-wash of an A-20 which took off just in front of
me. The turn was executed at a speed of approximately 125 m.p.h.,
being only a 90° turn and not exceeding double needle width. The air-
speed of the climbing turn did not drop below 110 m.p.h. at any time,
thus making a chandelle maneuver impossible in an AT-6 type airplane.
My statement may be further substantiated by General McMahon.

There is a possibility that because I was critical of the Palm
Springs Tower to the Airdrome Officer for failure to have transportation
to meet the General's ship might be the reason for the charge. Prior
to landing, the Palm Springs Tower was notified of our arrival. Due to
the fact that we were carrying a General and a Colonel, transportation
was requested to meet the planes. This request was not complied with
by the Palm Springs Tower.

KENNETH H. DAHLBERG,
2d Lt, Air Corps,
O-733838.

Ken's statement after the Palm Springs flight.

DESERT TRAINING CENTER • CALIFORNIA •

Hq. 77th Div.
APO 77
Los Angeles, Cal.
Aug. 31, 1943

Dear Dahlberg:

Just a note to thank you again
for the fine trip.

Gen. McMahon and I enjoyed
every minute of the time and both hope
we will be able to go with you again.

Sincerely,

Col. D. O. McNair

HEADQUARTERS 77TH INFANTRY DIVISION ARTILLERY
OFFICE OF THE COMMANDING GENERAL

APO #77   LOS ANGELES, CALIFORNIA

7 September 1943

SUBJECT: Flight to Palm Springs on August 29, 1943

TO   : Commanding Officer, Luke Field, Arizona.

1. This is to certify I was a passenger in the plane
piloted by Lt. K.A. Dahlberg, which took off from Palm Springs
at approximately 1730, 29 August 1943. It was a normal takeoff
and no Schandelles or violent turns were made.

2. I wish to commend Lt. Dahlberg on the fine manner
in which he carried out the entire flight.

J.E. McMAHON
Brigadier General , U.S. Army
Commanding

Col. McNair and Gen. McMahon's testimonials after their flight with Ken.

general, and he was killed at St. Lo in France when, because of bad weather, the Americans dropped their bombs on the American forces. He was the commanding general."

That final training stint at Luke lasted several months, but Dahlberg finally got orders to begin the second half of his military career, that of a fighter pilot. His first stop was in Leesburg, Florida, for six weeks of training on the P-47 fighter. The training consisted of more practice in dive bombing and gunnery, and also in getting used to a bigger plane. The P-40s he had been instructing in at Luke had 1,360 horsepower, but the P-47 was bigger. "There must have been a couple thousand horsepower, plus there were eight guns, four on each wing, each a .50-caliber. They converged at two hundred yards, and if you hit the target at the right convergence, you could blow a truck right off the road."

Ken visits the farm during the war.

The next stop was Camp Kilmer in New Jersey, where he boarded a ship and headed to England as part of a convoy. A week later he was part of the 354th Fighter Group, just as the Americans were preparing to land on the beaches at Normandy.

```
                    S H I P P I N G   T I C K E T
NO ACCOUNTABILITY PROPERTY                          AUTHORITY: WD Cir 405, 1942

CONSIGNOR: SUPPLY OFFICER, DALE MABRY REPLACEMENT DEPOT DETACHMENT,
           DALE MABRY FIELD, TALLAHASSEE, FLORIDA
                                          Date   4/25/44

SHIP TO:

      DAHLBERG          KENNETH      H.    1st Lt.,   0733838
      (LAST NAME)      (FIRST)    (INITAL)  (RANK)   (SERIAL NO.)


AUTH.  SHIPPED  UNIT  SIZE          ARTICLE

  1        1     ea.          Flashlight, TL-122-A (Complete)
  1        1     ea.          Headset, HS-38
  1              ea.          Message Book, M-105-A
  1        1     ea.          Microphone, T-44 or T-42

  1        1     ea.          Packet, first aid
  1              ea.          Packet, first aid, parachute
  1        1     box          Sulfadiazine, 20 tablets

  1              ea.          Mask, gas, service
                 ea.          Impregnite, shoe, 8oz.
                 ea.          Tube, ointment, protective
                 ea.          Dust Respirator, M-1
```

    I CERTIFY THAT THE ARTICLES LISTED HEREON(HAVE NOT PREVIOUSLY BEEN
ISSUED TO ME)(WERE ISSUED TO ME AT _____ BUT WERE
TURNED IN BY ME AT _____ AND HAVE NOT BEEN REPLACED)(WERE
ISSUED TO ME AT _____ BUT WERE LOST OR WERE RENDERED UN-
SERVICEABLE BY MEANS OTHER THAN FAIR WEAR AND TEAR; THAT PROPER ADJUSTMENT
HAS BEEN EFFECTED AND NO REPLACEMENT OF ANY OF THESE ARTICLES HAD BEEN RE-
CEIVED.

                        1ELt Kenneth H Dahlberg 0-733838
                        (GRADE) (SIGNATURE) (SERIAL NO.)
    I CERTIFY THAT I HAVE THIS DATE ISSUED THE ITEMS LISTED HEREON TO THE
PERSON WHO ACCOMPLISHED THE FOREGOING CERTIFICATE.

                        _____
                        SUPPLY OFFICER, D.M. REP. DEP. DET.

Just before he headed overseas, Ken was issued his flight equipment at Mabry Field in Florida.

Chapter Four

Into Combat

June 1944 was a crucial period of World War II. In the east, the Germans were desperately fighting back the Russians, who had gained the advantage in a series of brutal battles. Minsk and the Crimea were recaptured that month. In a place called Auschwitz in Poland, more than 9,000 people would be gassed and cremated in June. In Italy, the Allies marched into Rome.

In the Pacific, the Japanese empire was steadily shrinking. American Marines were invading Saipan, and in the Marianas, U.S. forces continued their punishment of the Japanese, culminating with The Great Marianas Turkey Shoot, in which more than 400 Japanese planes were shot down.

In England, as the month began, all was ready for the greatest invasion of all time. Great armies had been assembled. Thousands of landing craft were waiting. Hundreds of huge surface ships were gathered for support. Men were standing by their gliders and airborne planes. The global war had reached a fever pitch.

And, somewhere in the Atlantic, Ken Dahlberg was on a slow boat to Europe.

"I wanted to get to where the action was. I was anxious to get over there. It was an excruciating trip on that darn, slow boat.

"I had become very proficient in the P-47, and I had something like a hundred hours of training in it. So, I thought surely I would be assigned to a P-47 outfit when I landed in England. But my final orders were to

THE WHITE HOUSE
WASHINGTON

TO MEMBERS OF THE UNITED STATES ARMY EXPEDITIONARY
   FORCES:

      You are a soldier of the United States Army.

      You have embarked for distant places where
the war is being fought.

      Upon the outcome depends the freedom of your
lives: the freedom of the lives of those you love—
your fellow-citizens—your people.

      Never were the enemies of freedom more
tyrannical, more arrogant, more brutal.

      Yours is a God-fearing, proud, courageous
people, which, throughout its history, has put its
freedom under God before all other purposes.

      We who stay at home have our duties to
perform—duties owed in many parts to you. You will
be supported by the whole force and power of this
Nation. The victory you win will be a victory of all
the people—common to them all.

      You bear with you the hope, the confidence,
the gratitude and the prayers of your family, your
fellow-citizens, and your President—

                              Franklin D. Roosevelt

President Franklin Roosevelt's letter to the troops.

the 354th, and, guess what, they flew P-51s."

The 354th Fighter Group of the Ninth Air Force, in preparation for the D-Day landings, had recently moved from Boxted, England, in the eastern part of the country north of London, to Maidstone in the County of Kent in southern England. Maidstone was just above the White Cliffs of Dover and a short reach from the beaches of Normandy.

Dahlberg arrived in Maidstone on June 2, four days before D-Day. "I told them I hadn't flown one of those birds, and so they said I'd better have an orientation ride. On the ride, they told me to pay attention to the coast of England because I needed to get it into my mind. They said the weather would probably be junky, and I'd want to know where I was. So I had about forty-five minutes total flight time in the P-51 before I took it into combat. If the FAA were running the war, we would have lost it. We were not qualified."

Dahlberg was joining a group of veteran fighter pilots. "They were already a pretty experienced fighting group by the time I got there. Most of the flying was doing escort missions for the bombers." The 353rd Squadron, where Dahlberg was assigned, had been busy leading up the invasion, flying several missions near Caen. On D-Day, the squadron escorted the troop carriers, a job they continued to do the next day. In a second mission on June 7, the 353rd did dive bombing at Carentan to support the 82nd Airborne. The squadron then stood down for five days to get a breather.

Dahlberg's first mission, according to the official Army records, was when the 353rd Squadron started flying again on June 12, D-Day plus 6. The fighters were flying in support of the Allied forces trying to force their way inland. At 11:55 a.m., the squadron left Maidstone and flew a dive-bombing mission near Le Mans. Dahlberg was in plane F in the third wing. The squadron knocked out two locomotives, many train cars, and some German vehicles. The squadron returned to its base at 3:10 p.m.

"Those were what we called targets of opportunity. Anything that moved, we would take out, whether it was cars, trucks, trains. You had to be careful when you strafed a train because they would camouflage the tank cars to look like boxcars or cattle cars. You would have to stay back a little bit, because if a tank car blew up, you'd have to fly through too much debris. It was fun to hit the head of the train, because the steam engine would blow up. That was really fun."

A strafing run would begin at about

On the day after D-Day in 1944, Ken was issued his .45 pistol by the 353rd Fighter Squadron.

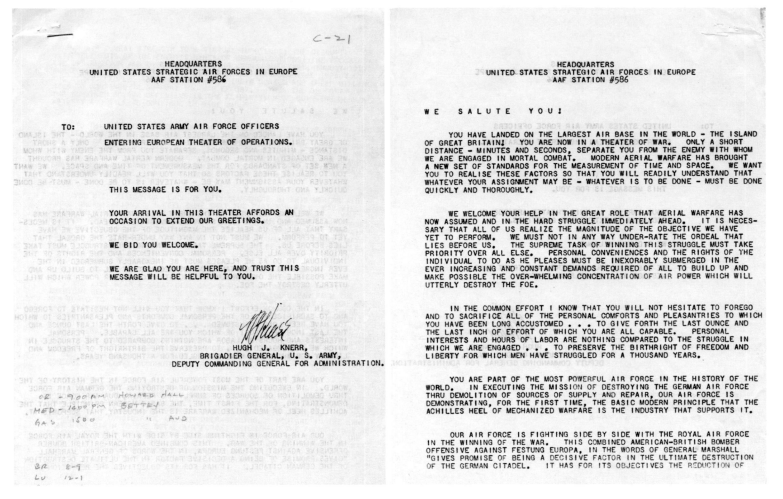

HEADQUARTERS
UNITED STATES STRATEGIC AIR FORCES IN EUROPE
AAF STATION #586

TO: UNITED STATES ARMY AIR FORCE OFFICERS

ENTERING EUROPEAN THEATER OF OPERATIONS.

THIS MESSAGE IS FOR YOU.

YOUR ARRIVAL IN THIS THEATER AFFORDS AN
OCCASION TO EXTEND OUR GREETINGS.

WE BID YOU WELCOME.

WE ARE GLAD YOU ARE HERE, AND TRUST THIS
MESSAGE WILL BE HELPFUL TO YOU.

HUGH J. KNERR,
BRIGADIER GENERAL, U. S. ARMY,
DEPUTY COMMANDING GENERAL FOR ADMINISTRATION.

HEADQUARTERS
UNITED STATES STRATEGIC AIR FORCES IN EUROPE
AAF STATION #586

W E   S A L U T E   Y O U !

YOU HAVE LANDED ON THE LARGEST AIR BASE IN THE WORLD - THE ISLAND
OF GREAT BRITAIN! YOU ARE NOW IN A THEATER OF WAR. ONLY A SHORT
DISTANCE - MINUTES AND SECONDS, SEPARATE YOU FROM THE ENEMY WITH WHOM
WE ARE ENGAGED IN MORTAL COMBAT. MODERN AERIAL WARFARE HAS BROUGHT
A NEW SET OF STANDARDS FOR THE MEASUREMENT OF TIME AND SPACE. WE WANT
YOU TO REALISE THESE FACTORS SO THAT YOU WILL READILY UNDERSTAND THAT
WHATEVER YOUR ASSIGNMENT MAY BE - WHATEVER IS TO BE DONE - MUST BE DONE
QUICKLY AND THOROUGHLY.

WE WELCOME YOUR HELP IN THE GREAT ROLE THAT AERIAL WARFARE HAS
NOW ASSUMED AND IN THE HARD STRUGGLE IMMEDIATELY AHEAD. IT IS NECES-
SARY THAT ALL OF US REALIZE THE MAGNITUDE OF THE OBJECTIVE WE HAVE
YET TO PERFORM. WE MUST NOT IN ANY WAY UNDER-RATE THE ORDEAL THAT
LIES BEFORE US. THE SUPREME TASK OF WINNING THIS STRUGGLE MUST TAKE
PRIORITY OVER ALL ELSE. PERSONAL CONVENIENCES AND THE RIGHTS OF THE
INDIVIDUAL TO DO AS HE PLEASES MUST BE INEXORABLY SUBMERGED IN THE
EVER INCREASING AND CONSTANT DEMANDS REQUIRED OF ALL TO BUILD UP AND
MAKE POSSIBLE THE OVER-WHELMING CONCENTRATION OF AIR POWER WHICH WILL
UTTERLY DESTROY THE FOE.

IN THE COMMON EFFORT I KNOW THAT YOU WILL NOT HESITATE TO FOREGO
AND TO SACRIFICE ALL OF THE PERSONAL COMFORTS AND PLEASANTRIES TO WHICH
YOU HAVE BEEN LONG ACCUSTOMED . . . TO GIVE FORTH THE LAST OUNCE AND
THE LAST INCH OF EFFORT OF WHICH YOU ARE ALL CAPABLE. PERSONAL
INTERESTS AND HOURS OF LABOR ARE NOTHING COMPARED TO THE STRUGGLE IN
WHICH WE ARE ENGAGED . . . TO PRESERVE THE BIRTHRIGHT OF FREEDOM AND
LIBERTY FOR WHICH MEN HAVE STRUGGLED FOR A THOUSAND YEARS.

YOU ARE PART OF THE MOST POWERFUL AIR FORCE IN THE HISTORY OF THE
WORLD. IN EXECUTING THE MISSION OF DESTROYING THE GERMAN AIR FORCE
THRU DEMOLITION OF SOURCES OF SUPPLY AND REPAIR, OUR AIR FORCE IS
DEMONSTRATING, FOR THE FIRST TIME, THE BASIC MODERN PRINCIPLE THAT THE
ACHILLES HEEL OF MECHANIZED WARFARE IS THE INDUSTRY THAT SUPPORTS IT.

OUR AIR FORCE IS FIGHTING SIDE BY SIDE WITH THE ROYAL AIR FORCE
IN THE WINNING OF THE WAR. THIS COMBINED AMERICAN-BRITISH BOMBER
OFFENSIVE AGAINST FESTUNG EUROPA, IN THE WORDS OF GENERAL MARSHALL
"GIVES PROMISE OF BEING A DECISIVE FACTOR IN THE ULTIMATE DESTRUCTION
OF THE GERMAN CITADEL. IT HAS FOR ITS OBJECTIVES THE REDUCTION OF

Ken and other new Army Air Force officers in Europe received this greeting.

five hundred feet. "If you're missing the target, you can see the shells kicking up the dirt. But if you get on a target, like a convoy, you can start in the back and keep going all the way to the front. You want to stay on it and get that last one because you know this is being recorded on the airplane's camera, and it's fun to see the pictures afterwards. But you have to watch the trees.

"The guns are fixed, so the airplane is a gun. You point the airplane. If you're coming in at 250 miles an hour, you really have to be on it, because everything is split-second stuff. You almost have to do it by instinct. You don't have time to figure things out."

The pilots did have a gun sight built into the windshield of the P-51 that would indicate to them the 200-yard convergence point of the six .50-caliber guns. The pilots, Dahlberg said, would use the sight as a guide, but eyeballing the target was still the preferred method. If the aircraft was carrying a bomb or bombs, depending on the type of bomb, the pilot would have to figure out the angle of the dive and the release point.

GERMAN AIR COMBAT STRENGTH TO A VIRTUAL IMPOTENCE; THE DISRUPTION OF VITAL ELEMENTS OF THE ENEMY'S LINES OF COMMUNICATIONS; THE PROGRESS- IVE DESTRUCTION AND DISLOCATION OF THE GERMAN MILITARY, INDUSTRIAL, AND ECONOMIC SYSTEM; AND BY THE RESULTANT PSYCHOLOGICAL IMPACT ON THE GERMAN PEOPLE, THE UNDERMINING OF THEIR MORALE AND THEIR WILLING- NESS TO CONTINUE TO SUPPORT THE WAR EFFORT. THUS THE OBJECTIVE OF THE COMBINED BOMBER OFFENSIVE IS THE ELIMINATION OF BOTH THE GERMAN ABILITY AND WILL TO CONTINUE TO WAGE WAR."

TO THIS END THE BOMBER COMMAND CARRIES THE OFFENSIVE TORCH; THE FIGHTER COMMAND SUPPORTS THE BOMBERS; COMPOSITE COMMAND COMPLETES THE TRAINING OF THE CREWS THAT MAN THE BOMBERS, AND SERVICE COMMAND SUPPLIES AND EQUIPS THE AIR FORCE AND REPAIRS AND MAINTAINS THE MACHINES INVOLVED IN THIS FIGHT TO THE FINISH. ALL ARE COMRADES IN ARMS, ALL ARE ENGAGED IN THE COMMON STRUGGLE WHICH CONCERNS OUR COUNTRY'S PRESENT AND FUTURE WELFARE. ALL ARE EQUAL IN THIS UNITED EFFORT.

YOU WILL FIND YOUR PLACE OF DUTY SOMEWHERE IN THIS MODERN AIR FORCE ORGANIZATION. I FEEL SURE THAT THE PART YOU WILL PLAY WILL MERIT THE FAITH AND APPRECIATION OF YOUR FELLOW COUNTRYMEN. YOU ALREADY KNOW OF THE FULL MEASURE OF DEVOTION AND SACRIFICE OF THOSE WHO HAVE GONE ON BEFORE, IN CARRYING ON THE SUPREME TASK OF THE AIR FORCE. THERE MAY BE LITTLE THAT YOUR INDIVIDUAL ACHIEVEMENTS MAY ADD TO THE LUSTRE OF ITS GLORY. ABOVE ALL ELSE, SO BEAR YOURSELF THAT NOTHING YOU DO SHALL TARNISH THAT LUSTRE OR DETRACT FROM THE SPLENDOUR OF ITS HONOR.

YOU WILL HEAR A GREAT DEAL AND READ MUCH CONCERNING BRITISH- AMERICAN RELATIONS. MOST OF YOU HAVE CROSSED THE OCEAN FROM THE NEW WORLD TO THE OLD FOR THE FIRST TIME. LIKEWISE, MANY OF YOU ARE AWAY FROM YOUR HOMES AND LOVED ONES FOR THE FIRST TIME. IN THESE TRYING DAYS IT IS YOUR DUTY TO NURTURE ALL THOSE PERSONAL AND SOCIAL RELATIONSHIPS WHICH REINFORCE OUR ALLIED PEOPLES AND OURSELVES WITH MUTUAL REGARD. THE ESSENCE OF GOOD BRITISH-AMERICAN RELATIONS BOILS DOWN TO THE SIMPLE PROPRIETIES OF - GOOD TASTE, GOOD MANNERS, RESPECT FOR LOCAL CUSTOMS, AND PRIDE IN APPEARANCE. I HAVE FAITH THAT EACH OF YOU WILL FEEL THE IMPORTANT NATURE OF THIS RESPONSIBILITY, AND CONDUCT YOURSELVES ACCORDINGLY.

YOU ARE FORTUNATE IN HAVING BEEN SENT TO THE VERY HEART OF A GREAT COMMONWEALTH OF NATIONS, WHOSE PEOPLE "HAVE BEEN BRED TO VALUE FREEDOM FAR ABOVE THEIR LIVES." YOU WILL RESPECT THEIR TRADITIONS. DO NOTHING THAT MAY OFFEND THEIR DIGNITY AND THEIR LIBERTY. IN YOUR RELATIONS BE CONSIDERATE AND NOT OVER-BEARING. YOU ARE IN THE LAND THAT GAVE BIRTH TO THE ROYAL AIR FORCE, WHICH HELD THE FRONT LINES OF DEFENSE FOR ALL THAT WE BOTH HOLD DEAR AND NEAR. NOW THAT YOU ARE HERE ON THE SPOT, YOU WILL SEE FOR THE FIRST TIME THE RAVAGES OF WAR THAT THESE PEOPLE HAVE EXPERIENCED, AND YOU WILL GET TO KNOW AT FIRST HAND OF THEIR SPIRIT OF COURAGE . . . FORTITUDE . . . COMPOSURE . . . AND SACRIFICE.

I HAVE NO DOUBT THAT, AFTER THE FIRST PERIOD OF ADJUSTMENT HAS TAKEN PLACE YOU WILL APPRECIATE WHAT WE, WHO HAVE COME BEFORE YOU, MEAN AND EXPERIENCE WHEN WE SAY THAT THOUGH WE ARE IN A STRANGE LAND WE STILL FEEL AS IF WE WERE HOME. FOR WE ARE AMONG FRIENDS AND BROTHERS-IN-ARMS OF OUR OWN, AS WELL AS OF A SISTER NATION, IN WHOSE HEARTS BEAT THE LOVE OF FREEDOM . . . JUSTICE . . . AND RIGHT, FOR WHICH WE FIGHT. IN THIS SETTING, NO TRUE AMERICAN CAN FEEL STRANGE. THIS RELATIONSHIP, THESE TIES, WERE NEVER SO IMPORTANT AS NOW. LET US STRENGTHEN THE BONDS AND DO ALL WHICH MAY ACHIEVE AND CHERISH A LASTING FRIENDSHIP BETWEEN US.

THIS IS MY MESSAGE OF WELCOME TO YOU. WHAT HAS BEEN SAID HERE HAS BEEN LEARNED THE HARD WAY AND I TRUST THAT YOU WILL BENEFIT BY OUR EXPERIENCE.

FAITHFULLY YOURS,

HUGH J. KNERR
BRIGADIER GENERAL, U.S. ARMY
DEPUTY COMMANDING GENERAL FOR ADMINISTRATION

"As soon as you released, you had to pull up. You had to do a severe, abrupt climbing turn. One of the dangers was that if you waited a couple of seconds too long, you went in right with the bomb. We lost a few planes like that."

The main danger was anti-aircraft fire. "They had 20-millimeter and 40-millimeter, and it was just like it was raining upside down. Their airfields were heavily, heavily defended, and so if you were strafing an aerodrome, the odds were against you.

"Fighter pilots went through three stages. Number one, from the time they soloed, they thought they were the best pilot in the sky. They got that sort of cockiness that was part of the fighter-pilot culture. For in- stance, they would take the wiring out of the stiff officers' cap so it looked like a crushed hat. You just had to have a crushed hat. That was our attitude: You can't get me. Then, after they see a few of their buddies go down, they enter stage two, which was, 'Well, maybe they can get me.' And then there was stage three, which was, 'Aw, shit, they did get me.'"

Attitude was important. Dahlberg allowed that when the pilots went to town they carried that invincible demeanor with them. Asked how long it took before an average fighter pilot told a beautiful, young wom-

354th Fighter Group

The 354th Fighter Group's history reaches back to 1942, when the War Department established a headquarters for the single-engine unit at Hamilton Field in California. The group was activated on November 15, and had three squadrons, the 353rd, 355th and 356th.

In January 1943, the group received the Bell P-39 Airacobra aircraft, and they began to practice the rigors of war, including aerial gunnery, flying in formation, ground gunnery, dive bombing and night flying. The P-39 was considered a fast plane, but had a discouraging tendency to enter into a flat spin, a flaw that was usually fatal to the young pilots.

Training continued at Tonopah, Nevada, and then back in California. In May 1943, the group got a new commander, Maj. James H. Howard, a veteran of the war in China and proud member of the Flying Tigers. Howard was a hard taskmaster, but was respected by the men. He demanded perfection in their training.

The group moved to Oregon for more practice, then headed east to Camp Kilmer in New York in October 1943. They arrived in England in the early part of November. To their delight, the pilots in the three squadrons were given the new P-51 Mustang, considered the best of the fighter planes by many. Because the group was the first to get the new planes, it was accorded the nickname "The Pioneer Mustang Group." On December 1, 1943, the group flew its first mission.

The group took up residence briefly in Greenham Common, England, and then settled in at Boxted for five months. In April it moved to the Lashenden airfield near Maidstone, its last base in England. The field was just above the White Cliffs of Dover in southern England.

Most of the early missions involved escorting the big, American bombers over the English Channel to their destinations. It was difficult and dangerous work, since the German fighters had the element of surprise. Maj. Howard earned the Medal of Honor by fending off a group of German fighters attacking American bombers in January 1944. In March, the group flew a series of missions over Berlin as the Allies attacked the German capital.

By April, the 354th's mission began to change, going from the defensive to the offensive. Dive bombing and strafing were needed to prepare France for the upcoming invasion. The targets were often rail lines and trains. Ken Dahlberg joined the squadron in early June, 1944.

an that he was a fighter pilot, he said, "About thirty seconds." Which explains a joke that was often told during World War II: "What does a fighter pilot use for birth control?" Answer: "His personality."

The 354th Fighter Group did mainly dive bombing in those post-invasion days. They attacked at Laval, St. Lo, Cherbourg, Bayeux and other towns that lay in the path of the Americans as they advanced off the beachheads and into France. Dahlberg flew on June 14, 17, and 18 on dive-bombing missions.

On June 22, only the 353rd Squadron flew in the group, and Dahlberg was flying plane O, "Beantown Banshee." Because he was a replacement pilot, Dahlberg never got to name an aircraft or claim one as his own. He flew Mustangs that had been named by other pilots, and those pilots had their names lettered below the cockpit. Beantown Banshee had been named by Capt. Felix M. Rogers, who would later become the squadron commander. Dahlberg often flew Rogers' plane in those days.

The mission was to Chartres, about fifty miles southwest of Paris. Three of the flights bombed a rail yard, taking out several boxcars and tankers. They began their dive at about 3,000 feet and dropped their payload at about 150 feet. A fourth flight bombed a railroad bridge, causing great damage. At about 4 p.m. a group of Messerschmitt 109s was spotted at low level near the city of Rambouillet. The enemy aircraft came from below to attack the American squadron. In the dogfight that followed, two of the 109s were shot down and a third was probably destroyed, according to the official report.

Ken Dahlberg was in the fourth flight, flying on the wing of a pilot named Forrest, when the action started. "I broke in from the wing, and the 109 looked like a barn. I was so used to shooting at little targets, this was just like a barn. I didn't know what kind of plane it was, I just saw it had a swastika on it. I can still see the guy climbing out. One of the things that I didn't like about that, as I remember it now, was that I kept my finger on the trigger just a little bit longer than I needed to, and I may have hit this guy when he was climbing out of the cockpit. I didn't like myself for doing that, but I was a rookie. I didn't know when to quit. I didn't have to do what I did, and it always bothered me. I know he was trying to kill me, but it wasn't me personally, he was just doing the same thing I was doing. He was doing his job.

"I got so excited afterwards I quit doing what I was supposed to be doing. I remember his parachute opening, and I was so excited that I just kept circling and circling and circling his parachute. I just wanted to wave to him and say, 'You'll have to get yourself another airplane, and we'll do it again tomorrow.' But then the squadron leader yelled, 'Get back up here in formation!' And so I did."

It was Dahlberg's first victory. Capt. Glenn Eagleston, who ended the war as the group leader with 18.5 kills, shared a victory with Lt. Charles Koenig, and Lt. Charles Bickel was given credit for the "probable." On the way home, the squadron strafed what it could find, taking out trucks, cars, oil tanks, goods wagons, and railroad tracks.

If Dahlberg thought he was going to get a big pat on the back for his first victory, he was mistaken. "It was only a big deal peripherally. It was what you were expected to do. We would always congratulate someone after we saw the film, but you know, most of the guys were twenty years old, and mainly we'd just smart-ass each other. Like, 'Who do you think you are, Goering?' or some kind of smart remark." Hermann Goering was the leader of the German air force.

June 22 was a big day for the 354th Fighter Group in general because it moved from one country to another. The group packed up its tents, footlockers, tools, spare parts and everything else and moved from Maidstone across the English Channel to Criqueville in France. The new base was called A-2, and it was home for the next two months.

The field had been built in a hurry by the laying of pierced steel planking on top of a cow pasture. The ground crews and gear came over the channel in C-47s, large transport planes. Dahlberg's part in the move was to get his plane to A-2. "Someone else was responsible for getting our footlocker there. Everything we owned was in that footlocker, and we hoped that footlocker would follow and show up in our tent when we got there. And sometimes on a move, you had to sweat that out. You got there a lot faster than the footlocker did."

Every pilot who flew from A-2 remembers the steel planking and the mud. Dahlberg said taking off and landing on the planking was not that difficult — unless it was wet. "The problem was the mud that would ooze up through the planking and get on the wheels. Once you put the wheels up, the mud would get in the wheel wells. Then you'd get up to 30,000 feet and it was fifty below zero. The wheels would freeze in the wheel wells, and when you came in to land, the wheels wouldn't come down, and that was a problem. Sometimes you just had to circle for a while until they thawed out."

It was a wet summer, and through the flying and living in tents, many of the pilots had colds. "The worst thing in the world was to fly with a cold, and we all had them. When you came down from altitude, the pain was excruciating. Sometimes you'd have to circle at 10,000 feet or so for a little bit until you could get your eustachian tubes cleared up. It was cold up there at 30,000 feet, and in the pictures you'll see us all wearing sheepskin-covered boots even in the summertime. And, of course, it was unpressurized."

One benefit of moving to France was the elimination of Brussels sprouts from the diet. "Apparently Brussels sprouts grew very well in England, because we had them all the time. They're from the cabbage family, and it produces a lot of gas in the tummy. Now when you go to altitude, you know what happens. The gas expands. There were a lot of physical considerations we had to cope with, between our tummies and our ears."

On the base, the pilots would file through a mess tent to get their chow – which often included Spam, made in Minnesota by the Hormel Company. Each man was issued a mess kit consisting of a plate and some metalware. "You always hoped that the mess people were aggressive about acquiring local food. You got tired of military rations. But the problem was that the local infrastructure and economy had been so destroyed that there wasn't a flow. You didn't go to the market to buy, you went to scrounge. Everything was scrounged, and we hoped our guys would be able to scrounge eggs from the farmers. Now and then we'd have some eggs.

"They would often trade commodities for what we wanted. Salt was one. You can't live without salt, and the military had plenty of salt. And so we'd trade and scrounge."

The planes would take off in formation, that is, two at time, wingtip to wingtip. If the field was socked in — Criqueville was only miles from the sea — the pilots and planes would have to wait on the ground. When the weather lifted at all, they would often take off immediately, relying on their primitive instruments to help them get airborne and aligned in their flights.

"The theory of combat was that you had a wingman. The guy leading was looking ahead, and the wingman was checking the tail. His job was really to protect that leader. The leader would do what a leader has to do, and he could do it better because he knew his tail was being protected by his wingman. The one thing you didn't do as a wingman was abandon your leader. Only when the combat got hot enough — then it was every man for himself. Once you got into combat, if the leader was attacking the enemy, you couldn't stay on his wing while he was doing that, because you had three planes shooting at you. So when you get into serious combat, the theory breaks down."

Ken strolls by the "Parachute Department" at a tent city at an airfield in France during the winter of 1944-45.

Combat was made up of quick decisions. "The first thing you want to do when you're being shot at is change your direction as quickly as possible. If you can throttle back quickly enough, the guy will go by you. If he's that close, and you throttle back and change directions, he'll not only miss, but he'll go by you, and now you're in position to shoot. Of course, the enemy is doing the same thing.

"You're on the bubble all the time. You're either at full throttle because you're stalling out, or you're throttling back so you can get behind the guy. Then you throw the power on, and the engine coughs once. It gets ugly."

When it was all over — the bombing, the strafing, the patrolling — there was one golden rule: Don't come back with any ammunition. "We'd find something moving. If it moved, we'd hit it."

The .50-calibers the Americans used were one of the most feared Allied weapons in the war — when they worked. "Pilots would think the guns jammed too often. I'll tell you when they'd jam: When you're taking a turn at four Gs, that's when they'd jam. And that's when you'd need them most."

Crew chiefs would often hop aboard the wing of an incoming fighter to get a first-hand report from the pilot on the performance of the airplane. Ken taxis back on a field in France.

When the Mustangs got back to A-2, the pilots would be debriefed about their mission. Sometimes they would have to talk to a reporter from Stars and Stripes, the official military publication. "When we landed there would sometimes be a photographer there. And the reporter would want to know what you did, even before you went in for the debriefing. They'd want to take a picture right then because it was more dramatic if you're getting out of your airplane and soaking wet with sweat."

One of the high points was to relax later and watch the gun film from the mission. The camera was mounted on the right wing and would start filming when the guns were fired. It would continue to film for several seconds after the burst to record whatever damage had been done. Once back at the base, the film was removed and processed, then put on the big screen for the pilots and for those who determined who should get credit for an air victory.

On days when they weren't flying — there were about two pilots for every plane — the officers would sometimes head into town to try a little foraging of their own. On one of these expeditions, Dahlberg managed to liberate a car with four flat tires. Once he was able to scrounge up four Jeep tires out of the

Army's limitless supply operation, the car became the official squadron vehicle — transportation to town whenever someone got a pass. "It was our first restoration of the French economy."

A goal of the officers was to find the local evacuation hospital. "It was just more tents like ours, but they had something we didn't have — nurses. American nurses. Meeting places were established in the local towns, and then we'd meet the people from the hospital. We'd all get together. That was our social life."

The freedom to move around changed greatly from the time the squadron arrived at A-2. "When we first got there we couldn't walk twenty feet from our tent because there were Germans all over the place. I still have in my possession a nine-millimeter pistol I took off a dead German kid. I found him not far away in the woods."

There were no rules about drinking and flying, because there was no alcohol — officially. "One of the reasons we liked to meet with the nurses is that they had disinfectant alcohol from the hospital.

Ken made himself at home at Field A-31 at Gael, France, by creating his own snug little office. It featured a desk, map, bottle of champagne, a radio and a liberated lamp.

We'd mix it with grape juice or apple juice. The other thing we could get was Calvados, a brandy made from apples. Now, if you didn't leave enough time between the Calvados and the mission, there was always the oxygen in the cockpit. You'd put your mask on right away, and if you set it at one hundred percent oxygen, that will sober you up faster than anything else. I remember that was the number-one rule: Set it at one hundred percent and suck deep."

The only semi-official time alcohol was permitted was after a mission. "When you came back, particularly from a longer mission and a tough mission, you'd be absolutely drained, and I mean drained. You'd have both physical and mental stress. Sometimes in the briefing room, we'd just be shaking, and if the flight surgeon saw you shaking, he'd come over and give you a shot of Calvados. That's 120-proof on an empty stomach. Think about that."

Enjoying a beverage at the end of a hard day of flying.

The debriefings were where most of the intelligence was gathered. Dahlberg said that during the first few question-and-answer sessions, the new pilots would say they didn't see anything. After that, they would train themselves to be more alert to what they flew over. There was a desire to help at the briefings.

Dahlberg doesn't remember ever taking a map on a flight. Instead, the pilots would take notes at the briefing on a little note pad on their left knee. They would note the direction and the distance of the target. "There was a lot of by guess and by God there. The real marvel was getting through all that stuff and getting back. You had to stay over 10,000 feet to stay above the .40-millimeter from the ground, but at 10,000 you might be in the clouds. You just do your best, and if you can't get the primary targets, you get the secondary targets. You don't waste your munitions. It was our job to help stop the German Army on the ground. We just tried to soften them up a bit. By beating them up from the air, it made it easier for the ground forces to conquer them, if you will. Our job was interdiction."

Ken looks on while ammo handlers load .50-caliber bullets into the wing-mounted machine guns on a Mustang. Each gun took nine yards of ammunition, and if the pilot shot the entire load, he used "the whole nine yards."

Chapter Five

Tools of the Trade

The main and abiding technique of every fighter pilot on either side was to get behind the enemy. You couldn't do much harm until you could aim your weapon — your airplane — at the other airplane. The best way to do that was from behind.

Ken Dahlberg said every pilot had his own techniques and skills. "I only knew I had to stay behind them, and I knew that if I anticipated that he was going to pull something on me, I wasn't going to let him do it first. Sometimes when I anticipated an extreme evasive action, I would just slow down, pull back. That would keep him in front of me. There's no general rule except to stay behind them."

When the American pilots could surprise an enemy plane or group of planes, they called it "bouncing." It mainly meant taking the initiative. Initiative was part of Dahlberg's strategy.

"After the war I'd run into Jack Bradley, my commanding officer in the 354th, and he told me that I just wasn't that good a shot. He teased me a lot, but his point was that I was aggressive. I flew on his wing a lot, so he should know. He just said I was very aggressive."

On June 29, Dahlberg was again in Beantown Banshee, and the squadron was doing a fighter sweep in the early afternoon near Granville. It was the young pilot's eighth mission, and he was part of an eight-plane formation. Lt. Harlow Eldred was on his wing.

The group was flying at about 9,000 feet when it encountered a small group of Fw 190s, or, perhaps, the enemy encountered them. One of the 190s immediately got on the flight leader's tail. Dahlberg took after the 190, and managed to distract the pilot from his attack. The two began a death-defying spiral to treetop level. On the deck, they continued a violent series of maneuvers, until Dahlberg got the upper hand and shot down the German pilot. The dogfight had lasted about fifteen minutes, an eternity in fighter-plane time.

"Right from the beginning it was nip and tuck because the enemy pilots were all in the Goering Squadron. The nose of the airplane was painted yellow. They were the elite. Goering was the head of the German Air Force, and this was their elite squadron.

"The 354th was earning a reputation as an elite group. We were knocking down a lot of German planes. We were, as I've said, the first Mustang group. Before I got there, they had plenty of opportunity, when they were escorting the bombers, to get into dogfights. And so they had experience, and they were earning their reputation, but we were perhaps not as elite as the Goering Squadron. Those guys were good. Later in the war, we were going up against some pilots that were probably rookies. They didn't have very good evasion techniques. We'd call them 'gimmies.'"

The Goering fighter Dahlberg faced was not a gimmie. "I was on the bubble from 9,000 feet all the way to the deck. Both guys in both those cockpits know that it's either him or me. And they both have total confidence that it's him and not me. It depends on which cockpit you're in as to who was chasing who. It comes down to who makes the best decisions in those nanoseconds you have to make them. You can't think of survival. It's got to be, 'How do I get this guy?' You won't get the last inch of performance out of your airplane if you're not using the utmost last inch of your ability."

Dahlberg followed the German fighter to treetop level. "We made a couple of circles pretty much onto the deck, and I got behind him and I got some strikes on him, some good strikes on him. Some really black smoke started. He apparently saw me, or maybe he saw the tracers going by him, and he knew he had to do something, so he made a quick turn to the right, just a quick turn to lose me, but I was up behind him. I was going slow and I was able to get him as he made that right turn. He made a snap roll — it was his only chance — but somehow I stayed behind him, and I stayed far enough behind him to get my nose ahead of him. Remember the water-hose theory? You've got to lead him, you've got to be out in front of him. I didn't see whether he got out, but at that altitude it would have been impossible to get out."

In such engagements, a pilot will never look at his gauges or wonder about what the book says about the limits of his plane. "It's absolute feel. Everything is feel, judgment, visual sensation and spatial awareness. You've got to get that nose out in front. You know you have to have a lead on your enemy. If it looks like your shells are going right for him, you're missing him.

"I think the clock stops, time stops. This is the epitome of exercising the human survival instinct. We were taught in training that we would have airplanes that equaled the enemy's. You learn that you've got to jump a little bit faster and stay the course. The guy that slacks off for even a second is going to buy the farm. It's an indescribable experience to really use everything you have."

Dogfighting is one of the major psychological highs developed in the history of man. "Well, you know what adrenaline is. A pilot is maximizing that adrenaline. And you discover that you have a lot more than you thought. One of the things you have to be careful about was blacking out because in the tight turns, you're pulling several Gs. We didn't have G suits. You were just kind of on the bubble. You'd want to maximize your equipment and maximize your skills, but you could OD. If you're pulling three Gs, it means that all the blood has left your head and is in your toenails. It affects your vision first, but you also can't trust your hands. The body

"Little Horse," a P-51 Ken flew, coming in for landing at an airbase in France.

gives you plenty of advance notice, but you've got to pay attention to that alarm signal. The beginning of the blurring, the beginning of that sensation in your hands, the lightheadedness, or whatever, you'd just better back off a little bit. You have to be able to judge pretty early into the engagement whether or not you can handle it, and if you can't, you'd better get out of there fast."

And even if a pilot managed the incredible physical strain, he sometimes still came up empty. "Maybe when you get down on the deck you think you're going three or four miles an hour faster than the enemy, but, guess what, his bird is going faster. Pretty soon, in the haze of the low altitude and the treetop haze, you've lost them. Now, you pull up and say, 'Where am I?' You don't have a clue where you are, and you're all alone. You look at your fuel gauge and wonder whether you can make it back to your field or not."

If the pilot was in northern Germany, coming out of a dogfight and realizing that his fuel situation was dire, Sweden was always an option. But it was a last resort because the Swedes, protecting their neutrality, would keep the airplane and the pilot for the duration of the war.

P-47 Thunderbolt

Known affectionately as the "Jug," the P-47 Thunderbolt was a workhorse fighter plane used extensively during World War II.

Built by the Republic Aviation Corporation, the P-47 evolved out of a prototype designed in 1940, before America entered the war. Its maiden flight was in 1941. The designers were two emigrants from the Republic of Georgia who had fled the Soviet rule. Alexander Kartveli and Alexander de Seversky had as their goal to create a fighter with a very powerful radial engine that used a turbocharger to produce additional power.

The radial engine and turbocharger were large and resulted in a fuselage that was also large, and not as aerodynamic as many of the other fighters. About 170 P-47Bs were built in 1942. The major armament included eight .50-caliber Browning machine guns on the wings, and three attachments for bombs, one under each wing and one on the fuselage.

The P-47C went into production in late 1942, and 600 of the aircraft were built by Republic. The major difference in the new version was a bigger engine that developed 2,300 horsepower compared with 2,000 in the earlier Thunderbolt. Even as the C version was being built, the final P-47D began rolling off the assembly lines in Farmingdale, New York, Evansville, Indiana, and at Buffalo, New York.

In all, more than 12,600 P-47Ds were built during the war. The aircraft had a kill/loss ratio of 4.6 to 1. The fighter knocked down more than 3,700 enemy planes in air combat, while suffering just more than 800 losses of its own.

The 354th Fighter Group was primarily a P-51 Mustang unit early in the war, but switched to P-47s in late 1944. The main reason for the switch was to take advantage of the Thunderbolt's capacity as a fighter bomber. The squadron was shifting from escort duty to a new job, helping the troops on the ground.

The later versions of the P-47 had armor built around the pilot to provide additional protection. That armor may have saved Ken Dahlberg's life in February 1945, when he took a direct hit from a German .88-millimeter shell. The aircraft was blown to pieces, but Dahlberg's injuries were not life-threatening.

SPECIFICATIONS
Crew: 1
Length: 36 feet, 1 inch
Wingspan: 40 feet, 9 inches
Height: 14 feet, 7 inches
Power plant: Pratt & Whitney R-2800-59 twin row radial engine.
Horsepower: 2,535
Maximum speed: 426 m.p.h.
Maximum takeoff weight: 17,500 lbs.
Range: 1,600 miles
Ceiling: 43,000 feet
Rate of climb: 3,120 feet per minute
Armament: Eight .50-caliber Browning machine guns
Three hard points with a maximum of 2,000 lbs. of bombs.

P-51 Mustang

When World War II began in Europe, America was mainly producing two fighter aircraft, the P-39 by Bell and the P-40 by Curtiss. Neither was up to the standards of the fighters being built by Britain or Germany at that point.

Britain was desperately interested in purchasing American aircraft, and negotiations were begun between the Brits and North American Aviation. The Royal Air Force was interested in using North American's excess capacity for building P-40s. But North American had other ideas.

The company, best known at that point for producing excellent training aircraft, asked the British for a 120-day window to develop its own fighter. In those short four months, North American was able to design, build and test-fly its version of a fighter — the prototype of what would become the P-51 Mustang. There is still controversy over how much of the aircraft was designed by North American and how much was borrowed from Curtiss blueprints, but the result was an American fighter that was in the same league with other fighters on the world stage. The British ordered 320 of the new aircraft, and production began in 1941. The British accepted the first Mustang (named by them) in October of that year.

The U.S. Army Air Force took notice of the new fighter and also began ordering from North American. The earlier versions of the plane, though fast, were considered under-powered. Again, the British came to the rescue, installing an engine made by Rolls-Royce into the Mustang to give it more power, particularly at higher altitudes. The Merlin engine worked well, and it was soon being mass-produced by Packard in the United States.

The Mustang was considered America's best fighter in the war, and pilots considered it one of the best aircraft to fly.

The P-51D, used by Ken Dahlberg in the 354th Fighter Group, incorporated the new engine and other beneficial changes to armament and design, including a bubble canopy that allowed the pilots better 360-degree viewing. The 354th was the first to use the aircraft in Europe and the unit was called the Pioneer Mustang Group. When Dahlberg joined the Minnesota Air Guard after the war, he flew Mustangs. Over 6,500 P-51Ds were built during the war.

SPECIFICATIONS

Crew: 1
Wingspan: 37 feet
Height: 13 feet, 8 inches
Powerplant: Packard Merlin V-1650-7, liquid cooled, supercharged V-12
Horsepower: 1,695
Maximum speed: 437 m.p.h.
Cruising speed: 362 m.p.h.
Stall speed: 100 m.p.h.
Maximum takeoff weight: 12,100 lbs.
Range: 1,650
Ceiling: 41,900
Rate of climb: 3,200 feet per minute
Armament: Six .50-caliber machine guns
Two hardpoints to attach a maximum of 2,000 lbs. of bombs.

Overwhelming odds, sometimes as much as six to one, didn't stop the Americans from engaging the enemy. "Just think of the opportunity there. I don't think we ever calculated the odds. At that moment, it was just what you were looking for. That's why you were up there. Maybe you hadn't seen a Jerry in the last three missions, and if you saw a whole bunch of them, it was like going hunting. Do you want to see a whole bunch of pheasants coming up, or just one? No, you want to see a whole bunch of them.

"It was fun going out and shooting up the countryside, but the real duel was the one in the sky. It's just like the old movies where they were sword fighting, just one on one. It's either you or him. Hollywood made that exciting, and fighter pilots just picked up on it. Those duels would satisfy their absolute convictions that they were better than the other guys. It's just like a prizefighter who goes into the ring. He'd better believe that he's the best, or stay out of the ring. He knows he's better. He believes it. Of course, he subliminally knows that he'd better watch his backside, or he's going to get clobbered.

"Also, there's a certain zest to the possibility or probability of instant death. It gave a zest to life that you otherwise would not experience. I haven't experienced it since. If you wanted to codify, or isolate, or define what made a fighter pilot tick, that was part of it."

A few days after Dahlberg's tangle with the Goering fighter, the 354th Fighter Group had its most distinguished passenger. Gen. Pete Quesada, the commander of the Ninth Air Force, showed up on July 4 with Gen. Dwight Eisenhower in tow. Eisenhower, of course, was the supreme commander of all the Allied forces in Europe, and he wanted to go flying and reconnoiter the battlefield in front of him. As it happened, the 355th Squadron, a sister squadron of Dahlberg's 353rd, had a Mustang that had been altered somewhat.

The mechanics had taken an old P-51 and removed a fuel tank from behind the pilot. They installed a bucket seat in its place and created one of the few Mustangs, if not the only one in Europe, with a passenger seat. Quesada took the controls, and Eisenhower climbed in the back. Because there was no room, Eisenhower was not issued a parachute. It was academic anyway, because it would have been nearly impossible for him to get out of that rear seat. For one thing, the rear canopy had to be screwed down once Eisenhower was in position.

The flight, accompanied by every Mustang that could be mustered as an escort, went without incident, and Eisenhower was very happy with his daring feat. But he was later chewed out by his boss, Gen. George Marshall, for taking such a risk. The men of the 355th renamed the plane, "The Stars Look Down."

On August 9, the 353rd Squadron had one of its toughest days, losing two commanders in two mis-

A Little Horse Reunion

They embraced in the shadow of the big, gray fighter plane.

They had not been close friends, and they had not seen each other in sixty-one years, but their brotherhood transcended time and rank and geography.

Ken Dahlberg and George Chassey had shared a war and an airplane once. Chassey had been the crew chief for Little Horse, a P-51 Mustang that flew in the 354th Fighter Group, 353rd Squadron in Europe during World War II. Dahlberg flew Little Horse on a dive bombing mission on September 5, 1944, over Germany.

"It was his job to keep them flying," Dahlberg said. "It was my job to bring them back."

The two had been reunited at the invitation of Paul Ehlen, a pilot and collector of military aircraft. Ehlen had undertaken the reconstruction of Little Horse, made from 80 percent authentic World War II airplane components, and 20 percent new or reconstructed parts.

He had chosen the name and painting scheme of Little Horse knowing that his friend Dahlberg had once flown the aircraft. Chassey, in his mid-80s but still working as an Episcopal priest in Columbia, South Carolina, had become aware through the grapevine that still connects the dwindling number of World War II Army Air Force veterans that someone in Minnesota had

Above: Ken with "Little Horse" in 1944.

Below: With former Staff Sgt. George Chassey and the refurbished P-51 in 2006.

restored a version of Little Horse. He contacted Ehlen, Ehlen contacted Dahlberg, and in August 2006, the reunion was held at Flying Cloud Airport in Eden Prairie, Minnesota.

Chassey and Dahlberg recalled the various fields they flew from during the war. Chassey had been sent as part of the advance party to prepare A-2, the first fighter base in France after the D-Day invasion. "They just brought in the bulldozers, cleared out the hedgerows, put the steel matting down, and called it a field."

"A-2 was so hot, so dusty, we had trouble keeping the sand out of the carburetors and the superchargers. We were lucky we didn't lose more planes."

Dahlberg said that the ground chiefs were obeyed. "When the sergeant said, 'Don't fly it, you didn't fly it. You didn't want to kill yourself before the Germans had a chance."

The two veterans compared some war stories. Chassey recalled when a P-47 was taking off with two 500-pound bombs aboard, attached to the wings, and one of them fell off. "There was a hole in the runway you wouldn't believe. The whole rear end of the plane was gone. But the pilot was okay."

Dahlberg recalled the time he "pranged" a P-51 when he was coming in after a sharp turn. "That was the tightest turn landing ever in the history of the United States Air Force. But the plane did not survive. I knew I was getting behind the power curve, and you get that 'aw, shoot' feeling."

Chassey had joined the squadron when it was first assembled in November 1942, and he stayed with it until it disbanded in 1945.

Staff Sgt. Chassey's job began at 5 a.m. when he and one other mechanic pre-flighted the plane. "We'd check the tires, drain the sumps, look for cracks, make sure there were no hydraulic leaks, check the coolant, and make sure there were no gouges anywhere." Oil was critical, he said, and a Mustang would sometimes burn five gallons of its twelve gallons of oil on a mission.

"That airplane ran every mission without mechanical failure," Chassey said. "We could change out an engine in twelve hours."

Chassey was asked what the biggest problem on the aircraft was. He laughed and replied, "The pilots." In a mechanical nature, "I never wanted to change a carburetor, especially in December or January when it's five above zero."

Even sleeping was a challenge in the tents. Coal was rationed to a few hours a day. "First you'd put an old newspaper on the cot, then a blanket, then your sleeping bag, then another GI blanket and finally your great coat on top. Maybe you'd stay warm."

And then head for your airplane at 5 a.m. "You'd pray, 'Oh please let this thing start.'"

Both pilot and mechanic agreed that thinking on your feet was critical to survival in a war setting. "We just had to figure things out for ourselves," said Dahlberg. "You learn or perish," said Chassey.

Chassey said he got to do what few mechanics did in those days. He flew in a P-51, a rare feat since the combat version of the airplane only had one seat. "One of the pilots arranged a flight, and I had to sit in his lap."

Dahlberg laughed. "That means there was no room for parachutes."

Chassey said, "We did a lot of maneuvers, including dive bombing. My stomach is still over there."

Over dinner later, the two talked about their lives since the war. Dahlberg asked Chassey how he got in the ministry business.

"It was always on my mind. After the war I wanted to spend my time building life instead of destroying it. I'll say this for the military, it helped you understand people."

Chassey described how it was for the ground crew when the planes were due to come back. "After a while you'd begin to get antsy. Where are they? Finally you'd hear

George Chassey takes a ride in "Little Horse" with owner and pilot Paul Ehlen in 2006.

them, and they'd begin coming back, one by one. You kept waiting for yours, waiting for yours. It was a happy feeling when your plane finally landed. The first thing you'd do was hop on the wing and talk to the pilot. 'How did it go?'"

Dahlberg smiled. "Crew chiefs were the heartbeat of the organization."

"Our greatest satisfaction," Chassey said, looking at Dahlberg, "was to see the pilot come back."

sions. When the first mission started at eleven in the morning, Capt. Don Beerbower of Hill City, Minnesota, was the squadron leader. "The squadron was strafing the airport when Don went down, and we were just furious that he had been shot down. He was a very popular squadron leader. They asked for volunteers to go back and strafe that airport again, and I'll be darned if we didn't lose Wally Emmer. He was commander for one sortie."

Beerbower, one of the best pilots in the Ninth Air Force, with 15.5 victories, had led the squadron to a German airfield about three miles north of Reims. The 353rd had a good day, destroying six Ju 88 bombers on the ground and damaging two others. Beerbower was hit by flak, and was seen to bail out at about 500 feet, but no chute was seen. He somehow survived the fall, but died later that day in captivity. He was twenty-two years old.

Capt. Wallace Emmer, one of Beerbower's best friends, assumed command of the squadron. He led a group of twelve planes that returned to Reims to carry on the attack that had claimed Beerbower hours earlier. Over the Seine River, Emmer was hit by heavy flak, and his Mustang burst into flames. He climbed out, and his parachute was seen by the other pilots. He was badly burned, though, and eventually died in a German hospital in February 1945.

When the squadron returned, Capt. Felix "Mike" Rogers took over as commander. Rogers held that position for about six weeks, until his tour was deemed over, and Maj. Jack Bradley took command. Bradley eventually became the commander of the entire group. Rogers stayed in the Air Force and retired as a four-star general.

The pilots did everything they could to be careful in the chaos of missions, but collateral damage on the ground or in the air was a fact of war. Sometimes civilians got hit. Sometimes your allies got hit.

"I'm quite sure that I hit a Mosquito, a British airplane, one time," Dahlberg said. "I was chasing two 109s, and they ducked into a cloud. You tried to judge where they'd come out of the cloud, and you tried to be ready for them. As they came out, I fired and hit this bird, and my wingman yells, 'Mosquito.' He was just where the German planes should have been, and I shot him without identifying. That plane went down, and I followed him down. It was just before Christmas. I got back to base, and I had to go see the chaplain. I was really bummed. But the chaplain just said, 'C'est la guerre.' It's the war. He told me just to be quiet and don't worry about it. But I continued to remember it distinctly because I knew the consequences of what I'd done."

As the war went on, the American advantage in the skies increased. At times, Americans were shooting down five German planes for every one lost. Dahlberg said it wasn't because of the quality of the equipment.

"The planes were about equal, and, as a matter of fact, they may have had some little advantages. The difference was that our pilots were better. We had better training. As time went on and our best pilots and their best pilots were eliminating each other, you got down to those who weren't quite as experienced. That's where we had them. For instance, I had well over a thousand hours when I got into combat. I would bet that most of the German pilots I faced had a couple of hundred — maybe."

Ken flew Shillelaugh, the plane named by Lt. David O'Hara, a number of times. He took the plane on its final mission on August 16, 1944.

Chapter Six

Shot Down the First Time

August 16, 1944, was one of the busiest days of the war for the 354th Fighter Group. By day's end, it had shot down thirteen enemy aircraft and lost four of its own.

From the mission report: "15-minute fight ensued from 11,000 ft. to deck. E/A (enemy aircraft) were aggressive and pilots seemed more experienced than most previously encountered. Most E/A tried to turn with us, a few tried to outdive us, none tried to outclimb our a/c. E/A were dispersed, and both our flights reformed when supply of Me 109s was exhausted. We destroyed 11 and damaged 2. Lts. C.E. Brown and Dahlberg missing; Lt. Brown believed to have bailed out." The report is silent on whether anybody saw Dahlberg bail out.

The pace of the war had picked up considerably in August. The German Army had been giving up ground grudgingly after D-Day as the Allies tried to advance through the hedgerow country. After the breakthrough at St. Lo, the Third Army moved into high gear, racing across eastern France. The Ninth Air Force was a key player in the advance.

Returning from a three-day pass, Dahlberg had arrived back at the base and checked into the ready room just to see what was going on. He was informed that one of the pilots was ill, and was asked to take his place. Dahlberg was still in his dress uniform, but he climbed into a plane. "I didn't have my sidearm, and I was still in my low-cut shoes. I didn't have my escape kit or knife. I didn't have anything."

The 353rd Squadron took off at just past 4 p.m. from field A-31 at Gael, France. The group had moved

Gué d'Aulne, the Baudoin estate, August 17, 1944.

there three days before from Criqueville. The new base had been a German fighter field, and had just been liberated by Patton's Third Army. In its rapid drive east, however, the Army had left many pockets of German resistance behind, some near the new Allied airfield.

Dahlberg was flying on the wing of Lt. Woodfin Sullivan. First Lt. Charles Koenig was leading the flight of eight P-51s. It was a patrol mission in support of the Third Army, and its destination was Mantes-la-Jolie, a city on the Seine River just northwest of Paris.

Dahlberg was flying Shillelaugh, named for the Irish weapon of assault, a Mustang that usually was piloted by Lt. David O'Hara of Pennsylvania.

At about 4:30 p.m., the squadron was notified that there were bandits at about 11,000 feet in the area south of Dreux. Koenig took the eight planes up to 14,000 feet, and the Americans "bounced" about twenty of the enemy 109s at about 4:40 p.m. Almost immediately, about sixty more German fighters joined in the fray, coming out of the clouds from the north.

Once the German fighters were encountered, there was no hesitation about taking them on. "So we went after twenty and all of sudden there were eighty. Was that a thrill. It's a good thing we didn't know there were that many. But you can only see so many at a time, you know. I do recall there were a swarm of them. When you're flying at that 10,000- to 12,000-foot level, you're going in and out of clouds, and you have to be very careful, because it's easy to be shooting at someone you shouldn't be."

Once the fighting started, Dahlberg was in the middle of it. He first attacked a German plane that was trailing a group of four 109s. The plane went down immediately, trailing smoke. Dahlberg found a new target in front of him, and let loose with his .50-calibers. The plane blew up in front of him, splashing his Mustang with oil. At about the same time, Dahlberg noticed his own oil pressure was dropping. He had apparently been hit. As he wheeled around and dropped altitude, hoping to make it back to his own lines, another 109 appeared right in front of him. His gun sight was covered with oil, but he managed to direct his aim by using the tracers from his guns. Another German aircraft was destroyed.

By this time, four German fighters were behind him. Dahlberg ducked into a cloud and was safe, but his engine quickly overheated from lack of oil. He bailed out.

Shillelaugh made a large crater near the Baudoin estate. Ken made a softer landing a few thousand feet away.

"The first thing you do is release the canopy. You want to slow down if you can. I had ducked into one of those puffy, little clouds so they wouldn't hit me. Obviously, you're a pretty good target when you're slowing down and you're not taking evasive action. You're pretty naked. Then I turned the plane on its side, and I unhooked my harness. Now, you want to make sure you're unhooking your harness and not your parachute. We did a lot of drills on that. Then you get out of the airplane."

Shillelaugh preceded Dahlberg to the ground, crashing into a field near the estate of Baron Denis Baudoin and creating a large, debris-strewn crater. Dahlberg followed a few minutes later, landing on the Baudoin estate, but a little more gently.

He nearly landed on Madeleine Baudoin, who, after her initial surprise, asked in perfect English if he was an American. There were quite a few parachutes coming down that day, and most of them were German. She told him to hide himself in a nearby pond because there were German soldiers on the estate.

Dahlberg hid among the bullrushes in the pond. "I just had my head sticking out, but sure enough, not long after I got there, some German soldiers came looking for me. They must have seen my parachute coming down. I snapped off a dry reed, and I was able to get completely submerged and breath through it like a snorkel. It worked."

Denis and Madeleine Baudoin

Dahlberg parachuted into the 2000-acre grounds of the chateau Gué d'Aulne in the Rambouillet Forest. Owned by Denis and Madeleine Baudoin, the estate was part of the ancient royal hunting forest. Madeleine inherited the estate from her father, who bought the land after losing a coin toss in which he was required to sell his share of an American textile company for about $18 million dollars in cash. To his brief regret he had not yet managed to reinvest the cash before the crash of November 1929, leaving him the wealthiest man in France. During the war, the Baudoins, who were part of *le résistance*, hid Dahlberg from the Germans in a pond and the three became lifelong friends. Dahlberg and his wife, Betty Jayne, visited Gué d'Aulne many times, and his last visit with Denis was in 1998 when Denis was ninety-two years old. They had cocktails on the terrace overlooking the pond where Dahlberg had used a reed as an air tube, and Madeleine told her version of what happened on August 16, 1944.

Ken with Denis and Madeleine Baudoin on the terrace at Gué d'Aulne, in 1998.

"A servant came running in and said that my husband had been shot by the Germans. I was running through the gardens looking for Denis when this body drifted out of the air and nearly landed on my feet. My first thought was, 'This is my replacement husband.' Then I thought, 'My god, he's an American!' Denis soon showed up, since the Germans had missed him and he only pretended to be dead."

Over another round of cocktails Denis began recounting his story of honoring Dahlberg in an elaborate Parisian townhouse soon after liberation. "I told my dinner guests — well, my fifty dinner guests — that we should toast America for liberating our country. I said that Captain Dahlberg represented America because he personified the bravery and skill of America's best. I embellished…a little…and told them that when I found my uninvited guest I introduced myself as Baron Baudoin and told him I was with the French resistance. I told him we needed arms. He said he did not have his revolver. I asked if he had a rapier. He said no. I asked if he had a knife. He said no. I told my guests that this young American came to France totally unarmed, but in his shirt pocket he had not one, not two, but three condoms. This brave young American came to France not to make war but to make love."

The German searchers moved on, and after a long wait, Dahlberg came out of the water. He was met by a Frenchman, who happened to be Denis Baudoin. "He said, 'Stay right here and I'll be back.' He came back pretty soon and he had sort of a trench coat. He asked me for my shirt, which, of course was soaking wet, and he brought me up into the woods next to the water. He said, 'You'll have to stay here because the Germans are still in the house.' The German commanders were staying temporarily in his chateau.

The Baudoins made several photographs chronicling Ken's stay with them, including a view of this hut where Ken stayed the night.

"The next morning he brought me my shirt back, and he brought me some bread and wine. The shirt was not only washed, but it was neatly ironed. He left promptly, and I was just sitting there on a log. I felt something in my shirt pocket, and took it out. It was wrapped in some French newspaper. I unwrapped it, and it was three contraceptives. Now, when you go on a three-day pass, it was Army policy to issue you three contraceptives. But I was a good Lutheran boy, and I came back from my pass with all three in my pocket. When the laundress, a young eighteen-year-old girl, found them, she carefully repackaged them in this newspaper and put them back in my perfectly ironed shirt pocket. I didn't know if that enhanced or degraded my reputation in France. I was really embarrassed."

By this time, the Germans had left the chateau, and Dahlberg was invited into the main house. It was a nice change from the woods, although he did have to puzzle out the bidet next to his room. Baudoin had saved some of his wine cellar from the Germans by walling it off from the rest of the basement. That night when the family gathered for dinner, Baudoin told him that he was breaking open the last bottle from a particular vintage. "I don't know what kind of wine it was, except that it was red and it was in harmony with my red corpuscles."

During the following days, Dahlberg and his hosts plotted an escape back to the American lines, estimated to be about forty miles away. "I broke the first rule of a downed airman, and I changed into civilian clothes. We were told never to do that, because if you're caught, they'll shoot you immediately as a spy. They dressed

Ken with Madeleine Baudoin during his first stay at Gué d'Aulne. Contrary to military orders, Ken dressed in civilian clothing for his escape.

me in plus fours and a white, civilian shirt. I don't know what happened to my uniform. They put a towel around my head, and they put some ketchup or some kind of red sauce on it to look like I was bleeding. Denis told me that we'd be going through some checkpoints and passing a lot of German soldiers, because they're retreating. The roads were jammed with horse-drawn wagons, and stalled cars and general chaos, but the Germans were still in control.

"Denis told me that if they stopped us to just play dumb. I didn't know a word of French. So we rode on bicycles like that for twenty or thirty miles. It was a long way through all these Germans and all that chaos. I got glancing looks from some Germans, but I played my part, and I lucked out. They had bigger fish to fry at that point. Finally, I saw an American tank and a Jeep, and we knew we were in friendly territory. I asked them how I could get out of there, and how I could get to my base. I did get back to my airstrip and went right back to flying, just like nothing had happened. That was a good thing. You didn't have to go through all the folderol of retraining or flying check rides to see if you're psychologically prepared. You said, 'let's go' and you go."

Dahlberg did have to sign a waiver, because, according to the Geneva rules of warfare, once a soldier has been behind enemy lines and goes behind enemy lines again, he can be shot as a spy. He also went through an intense debriefing by Army intelligence. "They always wanted to know what anybody knew who had been behind the lines."

When Dahlberg returned, he also found out that despite not having any gun film, he had been credited with the three victories on his last flight. It made him an ace — with five kills — after only twenty-four missions. There was no major celebration. "We'd kid each other a little bit, but there was no big deal made about it. It became a bigger deal after the war. At the time, you have a different perspective. I suppose it's the subliminal excitement that's going on all the time. It was an incredible place we had in the war at that time. We were above the fray, but very much in the fray. It looked like a cleaner job than being on the ground. What we did was a combination of adrenaline and fear. We were moving fast."

Dahlberg's return to combat flying, nine days after he had been shot down, was not a triumphant one. "There was a fire in the wiring someplace, because there was heavy smoke in the cockpit just as I took off. I didn't see any flames, but there obviously was a fire. I had to open the

Ken and Denis Baudoin in front of the estate stables during a visit in the 1950s.

canopy, even though I had my mask on. I didn't know if I'd lose my mask at any time. Fire is the most scary thing on a plane, particularly when you're too low to bail out." Dahlberg landed the plane safely.

After the liberation of Paris in late August, Dahlberg and his squadron commander, Maj. Jack Bradley, commandeered a Jeep and headed there. Denis Baudoin, Dahlberg's host and benefactor after he had been shot down, had invited Dahlberg to a dinner. The event was held at a beautiful old mansion that once had been owned by a Russian archduke. On this particular night, Baudoin had assembled a who's-who list of Paris dignitaries so that he could show off his rescued pilot.

Baudoin told the assembled luminaries of the brave young aviator's arrival, via parachute, at his estate. He introduced himself to the American as a member of the resistance and said they needed arms. Did he have his revolver? No, Dahlberg replied. Did he have a rapier? No. Or even a knife? No.

The young American was totally unarmed, Baudoin continued, "but in his shirt pocket he had not one, not two, but three condoms. This brave young American came to France not to make war but to make love."

Ken's 1944 inscription in the Baudoin's chateau guestbook. The entry above Ken's notes that the book was sealed on Christmas 1941 on the death of Madeleine's father, and was reopened on August 18, 1944, with the arrival of the "delightful American parachutist."

Baudoin also tried to show his appreciation for what the Americans were doing for his country by renting a house in Paris that he converted into a club for the 353rd Squadron. "It was a city club, and he put furniture in it and stocked the bar to the best of his ability. We had to do most of the stocking. It had three bedrooms and maids, and the idea was that anyone from the 353rd who came to Paris could stay there. It was his gift."

Also, about this time, Baudoin brought Dahlberg to the famous Paris restaurant Ledoyen for a meal. "There was a couple sitting at a table right next to us, and Denis wanted me to meet them. The guy was an American writer named Ernest, as in Hemingway, and he had a date. His date was a German woman — well, an American movie actress with a German background. Her name was Marlene Dietrich. Denis knew these people well, and I didn't know them at all. I was just a country kid. I'd never heard of Ernest Hemingway."

The 354th Fighter Group was active through the end of August and early September, supporting the American dash across France. Most of the missions were dive bombing or fighter sweeps. On September 12, Dahlberg had one of the most productive missions flown by any pilot in the European theater.

It was his thirty-first mission, and Dahlberg was flying the Mustang lettered "N," part of a fourteen-plane formation headed for Frankfurt. Lt. Andrew Ritchie was on his wing, and Lt. C.E. Brown, who had been shot down the same day as Dahlberg, was the squadron leader.

The mission was a fighter sweep, and it arrived over Koblenz about noon. Two of the flights strafed Limburg Airfield, destroying a number of German planes, while the third flight stayed aloft, providing top cover. The group then flew on to Frankfurt and, flying at 9,000 feet, bounced a large group of Fw 190s flying at about 7,000 feet about ten miles northwest of the city. There were more than forty planes in the German group. Part of the 353rd flew up to 14,000 feet to divert a group of 109s from entering the dogfight, and the tactic worked. Meanwhile, below, the Americans were doing well against the 190s. "FW 190s were very aggressive, although pilots did not seem to be very experienced," the official report said. "All stayed to fight, and most were shot down." The 190s were apparently on their way to attack a group of B-17 bombers when they were jumped.

Dahlberg was in the thick of it immediately, and downed his first two 190s with short bursts to the cockpit area. Both blew up with one burst of his .50-caliber machine guns. As he pulled up from the second kill, he got on the tail of a third 190, whose pilot tried to evade him by climbing. Dahlberg climbed with him and sawed off the German fighter's right wing with a burst. The German pilot bailed out. Dahlberg looked around for more action and spotted a 190 blasting away at a Mustang while the Mustang was busy shooting at a German plane. Dahlberg dropped down to lend a hand, and got some bullets into the 190's canopy area. The enemy aircraft went spinning into the ground.

When the fight was over, fifteen minutes after it started, Dahlberg had achieved four victories and was credited with damaging another German fighter. In all, the squadron had knocked down twenty-two Fw 190s and had lost two Mustangs, piloted by Lt. Robert Reynolds and Lt. Thomas Miller. Dahlberg's victory total had now reached nine.

On a practice flight September 19, Dahlberg had the chance to fly over the estate that had provided him shelter and an escape some weeks before. "I made maybe a half-dozen passes right over it, took a few shingles off as I remember. Madeleine told me later that the chickens didn't lay an egg for a week afterward. I gave it a good buzz job."

Apparently it was one of those days to have fun, and Dahlberg continued the joy ride right back to the base. "I was just hotdogging it that day, and as I came into the field to land, I buzzed the field right down to the deck. As I pulled up, and was going around in the pattern, I let my wheels down. Your wheels are going down at ninety degrees, but there's enough G-force there that they go down nicely. Then you make the tightest turn you can.

"It was a tight, tight, tight, tight circle. We were taught to do that, flying from these bases, because they were right up against the enemy. At one of these bases, and I think it was Gael, you had to be careful they weren't shooting at you while you were still in the pattern. They were that close. So you had to stay tight, but this time I was hotdogging it, and I just overdid it. It got away from me and I just plain stalled in, and I was lucky to keep it straight, but it mushed, stalled, mushed, and sunk right in. I think the wheel struts came up into the wings. It was bad."

In the parlance of the Army Air Force, Dahlberg had "pranged" his Mustang. He later said it was the "second dumbest" act of his military career, only trailing the flight under the wires, or almost under the wires, at the Colorado River when he was a flight instructor. The pranging, since it happened right at the base, led to a blizzard of paperwork and to a statement by Dahlberg admitting his guilt. The Army didn't like to

lose one of its $90,000 airplanes.

The official report attributed the accident to "100% pilot error," and added this recommendation: "That pilots, as they become more experienced, be repeatedly cautioned about over-confidence and laxity in pilot technique. It should be brought to the attention of all pilots that the airplane still has to be flown, regardless of how much experience he might have." In Dahlberg's signed statement, he noted, "It is my opinion this accident was caused by poor pilot technique."

Ken, at right, and other officers from his group visited the Ninth Air Force Headquarters in Paris. 353rd Squadron Commander Mike Rogers is on the left.

"I think the whole thing went into my 201 file, and probably cost me a promotion or two."

On November 4, on his thirty-eighth mission, Dahlberg for the first time was a flight leader on a run to Neukirchen escorting B-17 bombers. From that point on, he was nearly always a flight leader and was frequently the squadron leader.

The middle of November brought problems to the 354th. The group had moved from A-31 at Gael to A-66 at Orconte in late September, and the weather had become rainy in November. The Marne River had overflowed, flooding the Orconte airfield. Buildings were literally washed away, and the tent area where the pilots lived was under water. The group was allowed to move to nearby A-65 at Perthes on November 11, but on the 13th, the really bad news came.

The 354th — the Pioneer Mustang Group — was informed that it would be switching to the P-47 Thunderbolt.

Most of the pilots were more than dismayed by the news. They were heartbroken. Dahlberg was of two minds. He had certainly had success with the Mustang, but he had also trained extensively on the P-47 and knew the aircraft well. The psychological problem for many of the pilots was that they would no longer be hunting out dogfights in the sky. The sturdy P-47 was better equipped for dive bombing and strafing.

The liberation of Paris in late August 1944.

"But remember, most of the pilots were nineteen years old. People asked me later whether I liked the P-51 or the P-47 best, and I said that's like asking whether you like blondes or redheads. I liked them both. The P-51 was a little slipperier, a little trickier. It was the one I'd want in a dogfight. But the P-47 was a wonderful flying machine. It went as high as the P-51, and it was little more stable in the instruments. And it did take some punishment. The P-47 was much more forgiving than the P-51."

The P-47 did have one advantage over the sleeker P-51: It had what the service manual called "wartime power."

"It was a water-injection system, and for some reason when you sprayed a little water in there, you got a little more horsepower. But it would only last four minutes. When you got back, the crew chief would always ask you how much war power you used, so he could do the proper maintenance. Actually, the crew chief never had to ask me. He knew I had used my maximum, and there would be no water left."

On the first day of December, Dahlberg was a flight leader on a mission to Zweibrucken to drop bombs. The 353rd Squadron was the only one of the group's three squadrons still flying Mustangs, and there were sixteen P-51s in the squadron that day. It was one of the last days the squadron would fly P-51s. It also was

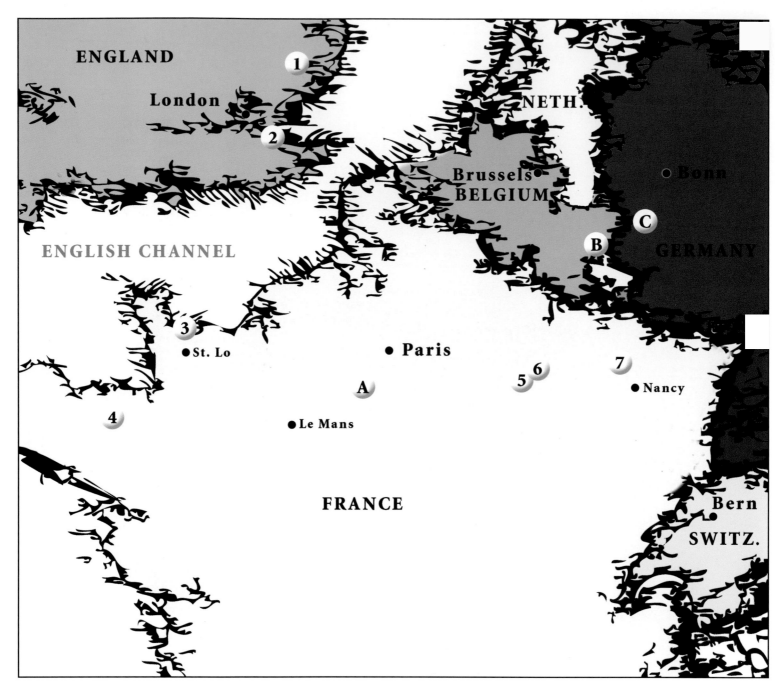

Airbases from which Ken flew:

1.   Boxted
2.   Maidstone (Lashenden Field)
3.   A-2 Criqueville
4.   A-31 Gael
5.   A-65 Perthes
6.   A-66 Orconte
7.   A-98 Rosieries-en-Haye

Ken's crash sites:

A.   Rochefort — shot down the first time
B.   Bastogne — shot down the second time
C.   Schwirzheim — shot down the third time

a big day for the 354th because it was moving from A-65 at Perthes to A-98 at Rosieres-en-Haye, a much-superior airfield. The pilots, of course, quickly nicknamed the field "Rosie in the Hay."

The mission went well, with the P-51s doing major damage to several trains in the neighborhood. At about 3 p.m. the squadron was attacked by two Me 262s, a German jet fighter that was new on the scene. Dahlberg couldn't remember if it was on this flight or another, but he remembers his first encounter with the jets.

"The first time I tangled with a 262, I thought I had him absolutely cold, and according to the film afterwards, I did have him cold. But nothing happened. We were simply not used to calculating those speeds. If we'd take a thirty-degree deflection shot on a regular fighter, the shells would converge on the target. But this guy was going twice as fast, and we didn't know it. If I had been briefed on the 262, I either was nodding or snoozing, because I thought I had this guy dead cold, and suddenly he's making this big turn so fast that I can't keep up with him, and now he's shooting at me. Now I'm skidding, losing speed, and he goes right by me, and now I've got a shot at him again. I missed him again. Our K-14 sight was not calibrated for that speed.

"If the Germans would have had a little more time with those jet fighters, we would have been in big trouble, because there's just no way to defend yourself."

Lt. Omer Culbertson, left, of Minneapolis, handed out cigars to signify the arrival of a baby back home. Ken and Lt. John Miller were the recipients in this publicity photo. The car in the background was one that Ken liberated from a French village.

Not long after its tangle with the 262s that day, the squadron ran into about thirty 109s over Karlsruhe. A dogfight ensued, and Dahlberg, on his forty-fourth mission, shot down two 109s, bringing his victory total to eleven. Dahlberg said the flak cars on the trains, firing 20-millimeter cannons, were deadly.

"The 20-millimeters would get up to about 5,000 or 6,000 feet, and if you got within that, you were doing it at your own peril. Everything was disguised. You'd think it was a cattle car or what they called a goods wagon, and all of sudden they're just blinking. The rounds blink when they leave the cannon muzzle. You know you're in somebody's sight."

The American planes would carry two 500-pound bombs on some missions, and the bombs could be of the incendiary or fragmentation variety. "This was the early days of napalm, and that stuff is wicked. When it hits, it's just a big, instant fire. Our mission was to support the ground troops, and the more enemy ground troops we could take out, the easier it was for our guys. That's why they called it the Army Air Force. We were part of the Army. You're supposed to take out all of the opposition, and the most lethal opposition, of course, is a human being. These bombs made an enormous fire, whatever the target was, and it was gruesome and awesome."

At this time, Gen. Patton paid a visit to the 354th, and the pilots and crews were assembled for his oration. Dahlberg was flying and was not present, but he heard about it later. "Patton started by putting down the fighter pilots and said that all we wanted to do was wear our crushed hats and chase women. I was told that it got very uncomfortable in that room. He was such a big name and his presence was so overpowering that the pilots were just shrinking in their chairs. And then he said, 'Well, if you don't like to chase women, you probably wouldn't fight very well, either.' I was told that the room howled with laughter. It had a great stimulating effect on the troops. He left our squadron very uplifted, and that's what a general should do, inspire."

Chapter Seven

Shot Down the Second Time

Bad weather and other factors kept the 354th on the ground through much of December. On December 19, Dahlberg was a flight leader as sixteen Thunderbolts took off from Rosieres-en-Haye for an armed reconnaissance around Trier, Germany's oldest city. Trier was an important railroad junction, but the P-47s were looking for the headquarters of the 116th Panzer Division, a German tank unit. They were loaded with 500-pound bombs. Before they could get to their target, though, at about 3 p.m., the squadron spotted enemy aircraft in the vicinity and jettisoned its bombs. Dogfighting is nearly impossible with the large munitions attached to the underside of the airplane.

The Thunderbolts were at about 5,000 feet when they bounced two "gaggles" of 109s at about 4,000 feet. One of the groups of enemy aircraft had about thirty planes, and the other about forty. The mission report said, "Enemy aircraft extremely aggressive and stayed in fight. Fight took place below overcast layer while top cover flight was above with leader's radio out… Capt. Dahlberg destroyed four ME 109s and damaged one ME 109."

Dahlberg, who was flying his forty-sixth mission in an unnamed P-47 with the letter O painted on its side, said much of the battle was a blur of action. "There were so many airplanes in the sky, all you did was keep looking and keep shooting. It was really hard to keep track of things. There's no way for the human mind to keep track of things in that battle. And besides that, you're pulling several Gs, and your brain is starved for oxygen. It's like seeing an accident, and three people all have different versions of what they saw. When stuff goes on that fast, it clutters the mind, and that's why we relied largely on what we all remembered, and then coordinated that with the film.

"I'm not sure if I got that second one because there was another one that got in front of me accidentally, and I had to go after him. But I'm pretty sure I got that second one."

It was a vicious fight, and while the Americans knocked down nine enemy planes, according to the report, they also lost three planes, including Dahlberg's wingman, Lt. Chamberlin. "That was a big battle. The Luftwaffe was not about to give up. They still had a lot of life in them."

When the credit board heard the testimony and looked at the gun film, they cut the squadron's kills down to six, and gave Dahlberg credit

American soldiers look over the remains of a German command post after it was struck by a dive-bombing raid by P-47s.

only for three victories and damaging a fourth aircraft. His victory total was now at fourteen. They were the last victories the credit board would confirm for Dahlberg in the war.

However, in 2007, the Air Force Historical Research Agency, using official documents that supported Dahlberg's Distinguished Service Cross nomination for that day, restored the fourth aerial victory and officially changed its records. Dahlberg's total was adjusted to fifteen, and he became one of a handful of triple aces in World War II.

Dahlberg flew several missions that week, supporting the U.S. effort to withstand the German offensive at the Battle of the Bulge. The Germans had attacked on December 16 and had pushed a major dent into the American lines. The 101st Airborne was encircled in the town of Bastogne, and the Third Army had swung north to try and relieve it. For several days, the weather was too cloudy to fly, but on Christmas day, the skies cleared.

On December 26, the squadron took off from A-95 with bombs loaded on each plane. On the way to Bastogne, the eight planes were ordered to escort a group of C-47s and gliders over Malmedy. The transport planes were bringing much-needed supplies to the 101st Airborne. On that day, there were more than 5,500 American planes in the air, the most ever during the war. American airpower was what the Germans feared most in what was officially called the Ardennes Offensive. And, indeed, the battle went the Germans' way, for the most part, until the skies cleared.

American tanks rescued many pilots during the war, including Ken.

"It was the first and only time I shot down an airplane while I still had two 500-pound bombs on my wings. We were attacked by a small group of 190s, and it all happened so quick, there really wasn't much action. The first thing you do when you engage the enemy is to jettison your bombs. But we were just getting ready to do some dive bombing, and those 190s were there and they just kind of made a pass at us. I skidded my bird, and they missed me because I was in a skid. I wasn't going in the direction that the airplane looked like it was going. I pulled out of the skid, and one went past me, and I got him, and then another went by, and I thought I got him, too."

The operations report credited Dahlberg with one kill, and a half-kill that he shared with Lt. Ivan Hasek. Dahlberg also was credited with damaging another German fighter.

The mission continued as the squadron looked for German targets of opportunity. "We had orders to bomb trucks and tanks, but when we got down there, I was convinced they were Americans." Dahlberg was a flight leader, flying the P-47 lettered K. "I got on my radio and told them to abort because these were Americans. It was at about that point that all hell broke loose. I don't know if it was because we were down too low on those Americans, but everybody was trigger-happy. You had to be. If you waited for a second opinion, you were dead. That's when my engine was shot out, and I had to crash-land.

"I still have these live 500-pound bombs, and so I peeled off a little bit in a tight turn and jettisoned those bombs. I was too low to bail out. There was so much enemy activity, I didn't want to bail out anyway. I wanted the protection of that big airplane around me. I went in with my wheels up. At the edge of the woods, there was a little opening, just these little saplings. All you can do is the best you can do. There was probably two or three feet of snow, and I was still going about a hundred miles an hour, so it probably gave me kind of a cushion. I just tried to make sure the nose was high so that I wouldn't somersault. I tried to keep the tail low and skid the tail, and then kind of flop it down. I kind of chewed off a couple hundred yards of those small sapling trees with that big, old P-47. Finally I coasted to a stop. It probably was the seatbelt that cracked my ribs. Obviously, there's a tremendous G force, a negative G force, when you go from one hundred miles an hour to zero in a couple hundred yards.

"I had crawled out of the cockpit, and I was standing on the wing. The other wing was smashed to pieces. I had my left hand holding my ribs, and I had my .45 in my right hand. I thought I was in enemy territory."

He was correct. He was about two miles behind enemy lines, but an American tank commanded by Sgt. Martin Dardis saw the P-47 slide in for the landing. The tank commander first used a Jeep and then went on foot through the snow to see if he could rescue the pilot. When he arrived, Dahlberg was perched on the wing.

"He said he was an American, but it sounded like he had a German accent or something. So I challenged him for the code word of the day. He told me I should just get my butt into the Jeep. He said, 'I don't know the code of the day, but if you want to get out of this you'd better get in here. And so I did."

The Jeep took them back into the woods, and to the waiting tank. The tank took Dahlberg back to the American lines, and he soon was being debriefed with some intensity. At any time, but particularly during the Battle of the Bulge, it was very difficult for the pilots to determine with certainty whether it was an enemy truck or tank they were shooting at. There was a lot of finger pointing on both sides about friendly fire. Because it appeared that Dahlberg had been shot down by American forces, his was a story the Air Force wanted to know about.

"I certainly didn't criticize them for hitting me. It looked like they were going to be bombed and strafed. I was at the Ninth Air Force headquarters at Liege, and Gen. Quesada himself was interviewing me. After the interview, he noticed I was cold. He was wearing the new Air Force jacket that had the fur collar on it. He took his jacket off his back, and gave it to me. He did take the stars off, and said, 'You can't have those.' Before I left the compound, I gave him his jacket back. But I wore it for a while because it was cold. I thought what he did was a really decent thing to do."

Perhaps because there was no gun camera film, Dahlberg never got credit from the Aerial Credit Board for those one and a half victories he scored before he was shot down.

Dahlberg was nursing his rib injury, but he was back to flying two weeks later on a dive-bombing mission near Bastogne. "In those days, you didn't take X-rays or anything like that. The flight surgeon asks how do you feel after he gives you a slug of Calvados. You tell him you feel fine."

On January 16, after another mission over Bastogne, the combat mission schedule was signed by Capt. Kenneth H. Dahlberg, the Assistant Operations Officer for the 353rd Fighter Squadron. It was the only time that Dahlberg signed the mission schedule.

On January 22 and 23, the squadron was very busy giving support to the 12th Corps as it pushed the Germans out of the Bulge. Dahlberg flew two missions on both days, the first time he had doubled up in the war. The first mission on the 22nd took off at 9:45 and landed at noon. The second mission took off at about 1:30 and came back about 3:30. On that second mission, for the first time, Dahlberg flew as the leader of the entire squadron, a position he was to take frequently in the following weeks.

Flying two missions in one day was hard work. "Youth helped. The energy of our leadership trickled down through the whole squadron. We had to get this job done. We had to get those tanks and help those guys on the ground. They were in trouble, and we needed to help them. What keeps you going when you're exhausted? It has to be a passion of some sort. It wasn't the big picture of winning the war, but it was the passion of trying to do everything you could at that hour or at that moment to be effective. That passion was embedded in every person, every personality. That's just what you did. If you had another ounce of energy left, you used it.

Ken's family sent a card in time to arrive on Valentine's Day, 1945. That day Ken was shot down for the third time.

Chapter Eight

Shot Down the Third Time

On Valentine's Day, February 14, 1945, Dahlberg led four planes out of Rosieres-en-Haye to Schwirzheim, near Metz. They were carrying bombs, and their goal was to take out railroad rolling stock. The small squadron destroyed twenty-five box cars and damaged a factory. Dahlberg was flying the P-47 lettered O on his sixty-fourth and final mission.

The four planes were coming out of a bombing run at about 2:15 in the afternoon. "I remember the end of that flight more than the beginning or the middle. I remember saying on the radio, "We're back at altitude" or "We're on our way home," when all of a sudden I saw big puffs of big, black smoke. It was from exploding 88s, shot from that famous German gun. To think that you could hit a fighter plane at high altitude is pretty good marksmanship."

One of the rounds made a direct hit on Dahlberg's Thunderbolt at about 10,000 feet. A statement filed by Lt. Calvin Walker, who was flying on Dahlberg's wing that day, said the four planes were flying in battle formation. "The first thing I saw was the tail of Capt. Dahlberg's plane blow up and start to burn, and the plane start over to the left and spin."

Dahlberg agrees that the round hit the rear of the Thunderbolt. "It must have hit right behind me, because there's some armor plating of a half inch or something that protects you from behind and on three sides. It must have been behind me, because I was blown out of the airplane. How I could have been blown out of the airplane and the harnesses and not out of my parachute is a miracle. I was unconscious, and I regained consciousness at about 500 feet or so, because I just had time to pull the ripcord and make a hard landing.

When my squadron mates got back, they reported I was probably killed in action. They told me later that all they saw were bits and pieces and no parachute. But I must have been one of those bits or pieces."

Dahlberg has no idea what caused him to wake up at the last second. "Maybe it was the rushing of the air. I know that years later in a church talk I said that the Lord was saving me for something else. But my own personal take was that the Lord just didn't want me yet. He wanted to give me more time to clean up my act. He wasn't ready for me yet."

Dahlberg hit the ground hard, and he was bleeding where a piece of shrapnel or metal had been embedded in his forehead. "We had been briefed to beware of the civilians. They were worse than the German Army, because the army was disciplined and for the most part followed the Geneva rules. We were all soldiers. But the civilians were madder than hell, because we had not only killed their pigs and cows, but maybe some of their children. There was just so much collateral damage. We wrecked that whole country. They were angry, and they would kill you with a pitchfork. Sure enough, I did see civilians coming after me, and I emptied my .45. I don't think I hit anything.

"I ran into this woods and disappeared. After dark, I started poking around, and I found a German vehicle with a tow trailer attached. Then I heard somebody rustling around. I climbed under the tarp of that little trailer, and that noise must have been the driver, because the vehicle started to move. I didn't know where I was going. Talk about no man's land. After a relatively short time, the vehicle stopped, and everything quieted down again. I poked around, and there didn't seem to be anybody around, so I got out and started heading toward the river. I knew there was a river, and I knew I had to get across that river. I used my escape kit compass, and eventually I came to the river."

It was the Prum River in the Rhineland in the very western part of Germany. "That river looked formidable, but I knew I had to get across it that night. I was getting weaker because I was losing blood from that head wound. I took a branch and used it as a buoy, and I swam across that river. In the process, though, I lost my escape kit and compass in the water."

Once across, Dahlberg started walking. He had saved his shoes by tying the laces around his neck, but everything else was gone, including his pistol. "I walked the rest of the night. I probed the woods, and I thought I might be getting close to the front. The Americans were supposed to be only six or seven miles away. So I walked all night, and in the morning I came back to the river. I'd just done a big one-eighty and ended back at the river. I really didn't have a lot of strength left, and I had a choice of trying to make it in the daytime or hiding in the woods. I didn't think I could make it another day without food or water, so I started walking west again. I ran into a little road. That's where the German soldier picked me up."

The German turned him over to another soldier, who began marching him to a collecting point. "That's when the soldier laid down his rifle to take a drink of water out of a well. I grabbed his rifle and hit him over the head. I was in a little village, and I saw a car there. It was a Citroen and it had some kind of German markings on it. It was some kind of medical marking. I got in and started driving lickety-split to the west. It had red lights and a siren, and I turned them on.

Dulag-Luft. Kriegsgefangenenkartei.

| Gefangenen-Erkennungsmarke | Dulag-Luft Eingeliefert |
| Nr. 6449 | am: 28.2.45 H. |

NAME: DAHLBERG

Vornamen: Kenneth H.

Dienstgrad: Cpt   Funktion: P.

Matrikel-No.: O - 733 838

Geburtstag:

Geburtsort:

Religion:

Zivilberuf: Hotel Manager

Staatsangehörigkeit: USA

Vorname des Vaters:

Familienname der Mutter:

Verheiratet mit: ----

Anzahl der Kinder:

Heimatanschrift:

Abschuß am: bei: Flugzeugtyp:

Gefangennahme am: bei:

Nähere Personalbeschreibung

Figur: mittel

Größe: 1.76

Schädelform: mittel

Haare: blond

Gewicht: kg 72

Gesichtsform: oval

Gesichtsfarbe: blass

Augen: blaugrau

Nase: gerade

Bart: -

Gebiß: 1 Stiftzahn

Besondere Kennzeichen:

Front   Profil   Fingerabdruck

Rechter Zeigefinger

When Stalag 7-A at Moosburg was liberated, one of Ken's fellow prisoners broke into the German offices and liberated some of the personnel records — including Ken's.

91

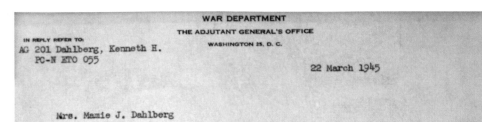

22 March 1945

Mrs. Mamie J. Dahlberg

Wilson, Wisconsin

Dear Mrs. Dahlberg:

This letter is to confirm my recent telegram in which you were regretfully informed that your son, Captain Kenneth H. Dahlberg, 0733838, has been reported missing in action over Germany since 14 February 1945.

I know that added distress is caused by failure to receive more information or details. Therefore, I wish to assure you that at any time additional information is received it will be transmitted to you without delay, and, if in the meantime no additional information is received, I will again communicate with you at the expiration of three months. Also, it is the policy of the Commanding General of the Army Air Forces upon receipt of the "Missing Air Crew Report" to convey to you any details that might be contained in that report.

The term "missing in action" is used only to indicate that the whereabouts or status of an individual is not immediately known. It is not intended to convey the impression that the case is closed. I wish to emphasize that every effort is exerted continuously to clear up the status of our personnel. Under war conditions this is a difficult task as you must readily realize. Experience has shown that many persons reported missing in action are subsequently reported as prisoners of war, but as this information is furnished by countries with which we are at war, the War Department is helpless to expedite such reports.

The personal effects of an individual missing overseas are held by his unit for a period of time and are then sent to the Effects Quartermaster, Kansas City, Missouri, for disposition as designated by the soldier.

Permit me to extend to you my heartfelt sympathy during this period of uncertainty.

Sincerely yours,

J. A. ULIO
Major General
The Adjutant General

1 Inclosure
Bulletin of Information

After Ken was shot down and made a prisoner, his mother received a telegram notifying the family that he was missing in action. This was a follow-up letter explaining the possibilities.

"After a while, I got to a checkpoint, where they had a log across the road. The log was just about a level higher than the hood of the car. I could see that, even though it was a medical vehicle, the guards were suspicious because on the other side of the checkpoint were the Americans. I tried to get around the log, but the end of the log caught the windshield and destroyed it. The car wound up in a ditch, and I was recaptured."

The Germans were upset about Dahlberg hitting the guard over the head, and retaliated by knocking out two of the flier's teeth. It was the only rough treatment he had in his time as a prisoner. Dahlberg was brought to a prisoner-of-war facility, and a German doctor was summoned to pull the piece of metal out of his head. The doctor didn't use any stitches, but bandaged it up.

"I was taken to a collecting point, and it was at some airbase, because one night I saw a German fighter. I wanted to steal that plane with a passion, and we probably could have gotten it with all the pandemonium going on, and because we were so lightly guarded. The rule at this collection point was that they don't have enough guards to guard you and so you have to be on your best behavior because 'we'll shoot first and ask questions later.' If I could have just figured out how to get up to the fighter — but it never came to pass. In the morning we started walking south to Munich."

The guards on the march gave the prisoners the same rules: Stay with your group. If you don't, you'll be shot. Some of the guards had taken Dahlberg's handmade English bespoke boots and had left him with some German footwear that didn't fit. "It was a wonderful pair of boots, and I'm sure they didn't fit the guy who got them. Anyway, I had to walk the next hundred miles in somebody else's boots. That wasn't very pleasant." The walking was bothering his feet, and he was still so weak from the activities of the past few days that he could hardly carry the knapsack the Germans had given him. "I dropped it, and I couldn't pick it up."

One of his fellow American POWs, a Jewish soldier named Spector, carried it for him. The march included thousands of prisoners, and the destination was a massive prisoner camp near Munich, about 200 miles away.

WESTERN UNION

M 26 Govt wux Washington DC 1004PM
5/15/45

Mrs Mamie J Dahlberg, Wilson, Wis

The secretary of war desires me to inform you that your son Capt Dahlberg, Kenneth H returned to military control.

J A Ulio the Adjutant General
955am

After Ken was liberated from Stalag 7-A, his mother received this telegram informing her that he was back in "military control."

"I was walking through the woods one night next to a guy from Norway. He had been shot down, and he knew a little German. They told us we could break ranks and get away, but that there were SS men everywhere, and we would be better off with our guards than with the SS guys. They'd kill you on sight. Anyway, this Norwegian guy and I did break ranks, and we went into the woods. We spent a few nights there trying to work our way back to the Allies. Being a farm kid, I knew how to find food, and so we headed for the chicken coop. You could always find an egg, and we'd suck those raw eggs. It was great food. Another thing we'd do was to squirt milk from the cows right into our mouths. It was fresh milk, really fresh."

After about ten days of moving at night and hiding in the daytime, the two were captured, but not shot, by the SS. "They must have been searching for us, because we were not moving at the time. So the first thing we knew, we had our hands in the air. They looked pretty mean, but they didn't harm us."

The SS men brought Dahlberg and the Norwegian back to a column of prisoners marching down the road, and they marched for another day. At that point, the prisoners were put on a truck and brought to Stalag 7A at Moosburg. It was a huge camp, filled with about 110,000 prisoners from every Allied country.

Meanwhile, back at Rosieres-en-Haye, Dahlberg's comrades were going through one of the time-honored

Stalag 7-A, Moosburg, Germany

Ken Dahlberg spent the last few months of World War II at Stalag 7-A in Moosburg, a suburb of Munich. (Dahlberg loves to say, "It was my first experience in suburban living.")

The camp was started in 1939 to house Polish prisoners, and as the Third Reich rolled across Europe, it became home to prisoners from Britain, the Netherlands, Belgium and France. Russian and American soldiers also became part of the camp's melting pot after they entered the war against Germany. Moosburg was in particular a home for Russian officers, and, by the end of the war, it was home to 27 Soviet generals.

The camp was built to house no more than 10,000 prisoners. But by the time it was liberated in 1945, there were more than 110,000 POWs in the main camp, including Dahlberg. In all, 26 nations were represented. In the work satellite camps around Moosburg, there were another 20,000 Allied prisoners.

The camp was liberated on April 29, 1945, by the 14th Armored Division of the U.S. Army. The division turned down a German request for an armistice as it advanced on the camp, but it did hold back on using artillery in the action. There were 30,000 Americans in and around Moosburg, or about 40 percent of all the American prisoners held by Germany. The division later took on the official nickname "The Liberators" for its actions at the end of the war.

rituals attendant to someone's getting shot down, when they knew he wasn't coming back. They were dividing up his stuff.

"When a pilot went down, all he left behind was his bed and his footlocker, and maybe a hanger with your jacket. All your earthly belongings were in your footlocker. Technically, the footlocker was to be sent home, but the regulations said the commanding officer would look inside to make sure there wasn't anything indecent in there. We had a standing practice among the pilots of 'Don't send mine home.' If there's something personal, go ahead and send that home, but don't send things like socks. Use them.

"Souvenirs, and all the goodies you collected, usually disappeared. In my footlocker was that nine-millimeter German sidearm that I'd taken off that dead German at Criqueville. Somehow that got sent home, and I still have it. One of my friends was honest enough to see that that one thing in that footlocker got home."

In the prisoner camp, Dahlberg was trying to adjust. "In camp, the only news you had was gossip, and the gossip that was going around was that Hitler was going to use us as a bargaining chip. We were supposedly the elite young men from every Allied country in the world, and we would soon be marched to the foothills or the mountains and used as a last trading chip. We didn't think we had a very bright future at that point.

"At some point, I was interrogated by a German general, and I remember him saying, 'Captain Dahlberg, we've been waiting for you, and why are you fighting? And why are you fighting against us? How long will it be before you are fighting the Russians? You claim to be Swedish, but you are really German. Your family moved to Sweden from Germany six hundred years ago.' He knew more about my family than I did, if he was correct. It did sound plausible, because he looked a lot like me. He had blond hair and blue eyes, and he spoke English with just a slight accent."

It was late February by this time. Dahlberg said that although he wasn't mistreated, the experience was not pleasant. "The biggest problem for a POW is loss of identity. First, they took your watch. You don't realize how important a watch is. It's a benchmark of time; it's a dimension that we subconsciously need to know. Then they strip you of any identity. But what really sinks in subliminally is the deterioration of hope. If you get sentenced to ten years in prison for some crime, you know you have hope of getting out. But we had no hope of getting out.

"Hope is more than an emotion. Hope is the underlying substance of the soul itself, and if you lose that, you lose your compass, and you sink into despair. All I can say is don't go there. It's not a good place to be."

The prisoners were kept in a warehouse-like shed, with straw on the ground. A total of 154 prisoners were crowded into the shed. They slept in their clothes. They never changed. They got to take a cold shower once a week. At one point, after being questioned, Dahlberg was put in solitary confinement for a time. "I wasn't very cooperative, apparently.

"There were no windows. It wasn't pitch black, but it was dark enough so I couldn't tell night from day. I was only in there a couple of days. I remember wondering at the time what I was doing in a prisoner camp. I didn't know where the hell I was, what I am, what caused me to be here. I didn't have a clue, except that I was fighting for my country as a soldier. The next question, of course, and one I didn't get to, was what was my country fighting for?"

There were few guards, but, as Dahlberg said, "There was nothing to guard." The men were shut up in the shed all day long. Two or three times a day, they were given a dark bread that the prisoners were convinced was half sawdust. On occasion, they would get a bowl of cabbage soup with worms in it. According to the Geneva Conventions, the prisoners were supposed to get a Red Cross parcel once a week.

"There would be chocolate bars and some concentrated something that Hormel put together. And there would be a sampler of cigarettes, because young Americans smoked a lot in those days. I had never picked up the habit of smoking, so I found out that you could trade a guard a cigarette for a turnip. And so we traded. Then we'd go a month without any Red Cross parcels, and the guards would tell us it was because the Allies had bombed the trains or trucks that were bringing the parcels. Finally, we got another one. Cigarettes became the currency, but the only thing you could buy were these turnips. They called them rutabagas.

"This was how I got to learn about inflation. The second time I traded for turnips, it cost two cigarettes, so that was one hundred percent inflation in one month. The next time we traded, I only got a half a turnip, so that was another one hundred percent inflation. In the end, the guards didn't have any turnips, and so that was hyperinflation. I learned economics in the POW camp."

When cigarettes ceased being a currency, Dahlberg learned something else. He learned how to smoke. "Where I grew up, you didn't waste anything. That was the number-one virtue of life, prudence. I couldn't eat them, I couldn't trade them, so I smoked them. It took me fifty years to quit. That was my lasting legacy from the POW camp."

The men would occasionally pass the time by trying to learn French, but basically there were few outlets for human activity, including exercise. Talking with fellow prisoners was the main activity. Unlike at the prisoner of war camps for Russians on the Eastern front, the Germans were not mean to the Americans. The poor conditions at Moosburg were mainly due to the fact that Germany was in the final stages of losing the war. The men were hungry all the time, and sometimes hallucinated. "You were just right on the bubble of existence." During his four months in the camp, Dahlberg went from 170 pounds to 120 pounds, but he saw no mistreatment. "It's strange because, on the front, you fight like animals. We all fought like a bunch of animals wearing camouflage and bent on survival. But once you're out of that, everybody becomes human again."

In the end, the war wound down, and the guards went away. "We just woke up one morning, and the guards were gone. We lived on rumors, and we suspected something was going on. Obviously something dramatic had happened, and the first thing we knew, there were American personnel around. There they were. Hallelujah."

When the first Americans reached the camp, they told the POWs to stay put and not to try to wander back to the west in twos or threes. The danger was that the civilian slave laborers also had been freed, and they were raping and pillaging the countryside. There was social disorder in the extreme. Dahlberg said the prisoners who had been in a stalag for several years obeyed the order, but the ones who had only been in a few months tended to head home.

"Another guy and I decided not to take their advice, and we did break away and went into the outskirts of Munich. We figured there would be an American vehicle coming along at some point. They were sup-posed to be in the area.

"We were in front of a house on a corner, and a lady came out and asked if we were Americans. She ap-parently knew the camp was breaking up. We said yes, and she invited us to come in. She said she didn't have much to eat, but that she had a little something for us. We told her no, that we had to get going, but she was so insistent. We asked her why. She said there were Russian slave laborers and they were on a rampage in the area. She said the Russians were drinking heavily, and she was scared to death for her seventeen-year-old daughter, for her safety. I thought to myself, or maybe I expressed it, well, how can you trust me any more than the Russians? I'd just been in a prison camp for four months. Why would she trust us two guys, the enemy, any more than the Russians? It put a whole new dimension on the meaning of the word 'trust.' She would trust us, but she wouldn't trust them. We did take her up on her offer of food, and then we kept going."

Dahlberg and his fellow officer eventually found a military vehicle and hitched a ride back toward the American forces. He found out where his unit was, but he was more interested in getting home. The war in Europe was over.

"Through the grapevine you kind of get pointed in the right direction, and I finally got on a DC-3 someplace and got to England. From there I somehow got on a troop ship coming home. I don't remember the name of the ship, but I do remember that I hadn't had anything to read for a long time. I got hold of a book by a Swedish author, and it was somewhat risqué. I was on the deck reading that book and trying to get some sun. I stripped down a little bit, and got caught up in reading that book. When I got to New York, I had to spend my first night in a hospital with sunburn. I wasn't in the hospital for Nazi wounds, but for getting sunburned while reading a dirty book. From there, I got on a train, and came back to Minnesota."

Ken with a new Cadillac, 1955.

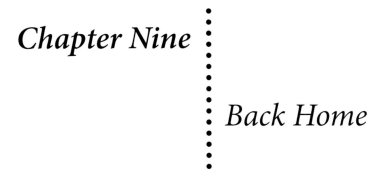

Chapter Nine

Back Home

Dahlberg had arranged a train journey to Minnesota that would take him through South Bend, Indiana, where he could see his old friends. While talking to his family for the first time in months, though, he found out that his mother was in her last days of a long struggle with cancer. He canceled his South Bend excursion and headed straight for Minnesota.

During the war, his mother had suffered with the uncertainty of what had happened to her children, three of whom were in the service. She had received three telegrams from the Department of Defense telling her that Ken was missing in action. The telegram that notified her that her son was safe "in military control" would only come much later in each case.

Mamie Dahlberg died in Miller Hospital in St. Paul, a week after her son came home. "There was a numbness about this stuff, trying to say goodbye to our mother. When I finally got back to the farm, it was not the same without Mother. Mother was the key to living on the farm. Everything revolved around her."

After some time on the farm, Dahlberg migrated west again to St. Paul to say hello to old friends. At some point, he ran into his old friend René Boursier, the chief chef at the Lowry Hotel, the man who had plucked him out of the kitchen at the beginning of his work career. The chef wanted to throw Dahlberg a party to welcome him home.

"There were eight people I had worked with, and for some reason we had the party at the St. Paul Hotel. The war in Europe was over by then, but not the war in the Pacific. Still, there was a lot of celebrating. I was still in uniform."

BJ and Ken at their wedding at BJ's parents' home in St. Louis Park

Another party was going on at an adjacent table, and, as sometimes happens, the two parties merged as the night grew long. The management informed the revelers that the dining room was closing. "The host at the other table said this party is much too good to break up, and he invited us all to his house to finish it. We did. And a week later, I was still living at his house. For me, I was just catching up a little bit. I'd just come out of a POW camp. This was so pleasant, and I was just having fun. I remember that his maid would come while I was sleeping, and she would wash my clothes, my socks, my undies and shirt, and then iron them. Every morning when I woke up, my clothes were spic and span. Finally, I guess I just sobered up, and I said to my host, Allen Hempel, 'You've been so nice to me, but I've got to get out of here.'"

Hempel told Dahlberg that he had spent the week observing him, trying to decide whether to offer the fighter pilot a position in his business. Dahlberg replied that the Pick Hotel chain, with headquarters in Chicago, was holding a position for him.

"He told me I didn't want to be in the hospitality business, because I'd have to work when everyone else lives. I asked him what kind of business he was in, and he told me it was medical electronics." Hempel explained that he made hearing aids. Dahlberg said he didn't know anything about medical electronics.

"He said I wouldn't need to know anything about it because I could start as his assistant. He made me an offer I couldn't turn down. So I got into the medical electronics business as the assistant to the president. The company was called Telex."

Just after he started with the company in late summer 1945, Dahlberg got his first experience of labor troubles. "Telex had moved to a new building on Eustis Street near the Midway in St. Paul. We were there only a couple of weeks before there was a strike. The strike was controlled by the Electrical Workers 1138 Union, which seemed like it was run by more communists than there were in Moscow. I came to work that morning, and I couldn't get in. I was still wearing my uniform because I couldn't buy any civilian suits. There weren't any.

"There were three or four goons in front of this nice, new factory, and one of them stood in front of me and said, 'You can't go in, there's a strike on.' I told him that I'd just got a job here, and that he couldn't stop me. I thought he made a pass, I'm sure he made a move of some kind, and I just, defensively, I thought, or preemptively, I hit him. And I happened to hit him hard, and I happened to hit him in the right place, right in the jaw, and he crumpled down in front of me. The other goons didn't interfere with me at all, and I just walked into the building."

Inside, Dahlberg found that there wasn't probably going to be a lot of work to do, because hardly anyone else had found the temerity to challenge the union blockade. "There were two or three girls in there, and one of them was the accounts payable bookkeeper. I knew her by sight, but I didn't know her name, which turned out to be Betty Jayne Segerstrom. I knew the mail girl a little bit better. I said, 'It doesn't look like there's going to be much work around here today.' And I asked the bookkeeper what she did on Sundays. She said, 'We usually go to the Thomas Avenue Beach at Lake Calhoun.' I didn't know where that was, but she told me. I told her that sounded like

Ken and BJ leaving their wedding for the honeymoon suite at the St. Paul Hotel

a great idea, and I'd meet her there the next day. I told her to bring her girlfriend, and I'd bring my brother Arnie. And that's where I got to know BJ, and the rest is history. We've been married for sixty years."

BJ had grown up in south Minneapolis and had attended the University of Minnesota.

"She had to quit her job at Telex because the company had a rule on fraternization. One of us had to leave. Her skills were transferable, so she took a job at a steel company. Later on, I always told the management people, 'Don't mess around with the help, because you might wind up with a wife.'"

Ken with his brother Arnie at Ken's wedding

Ken and BJ had a January wedding at BJ's parents' home. They moved into the honeymoon suite at the St. Paul Hotel, but in the morning they saw the price on the back of the door and promptly checked out. They headed back to the sparsely furnished one-bedroom home they had just bought in New Brighton. They had bought the home with $1000 borrowed from Ken's brother Mervin and a bank mortgage very reluctantly given because the banker thought that New Brighton was suitable only for pig farming.

They went for a long afternoon walk on the bitter January day, underdressed for the weather, and they spent the rest of their honeymoon taking care of each other's colds.

Not long after starting with Telex, Dahlberg found out that the Minnesota Air National Guard was being reactivated. Not only that, but it was flying Mustangs. Dahlberg quickly became a weekend warrior.

"When I was on duty, I was wearing these big Army Air Corps headsets. But when I'd come back to work, I'd see all these electronic parts — little speakers and microphones. I just had an idea that we could make a better headset."

Dahlberg was able to convince Hempel to get Telex into the electro-acoustic business. The pilot met with Telex's engineers, and the company soon produced the first miniaturized headset. Telex is still a major manufacturer of military and other aviation headsets.

Another Dahlberg idea was the pillow speaker for hospitals. In those days, with the radio in common usage, many patients would bring one to keep them company in their hospital bed. In an open ward, the cacophony of radio stations made the hospital a chaotic place. The solution, as Dahlberg saw it, was to install a radio set with a coin slot in it, similar to a parking meter, then have the sound come out in a speaker that would go beneath the pillow. Everyone in the ward, for ten cents per hour, could have his or her own radio entertainment and not disturb their neighbors.

Dahlberg found a local radio manufacturer in New Brighton, Minnesota, to create a model of the pillow-speaker concept. "I presented this idea to my boss, and he told me that I was getting out of the business the company was in. I wasn't doing anything behind my boss' back. I had been talking to him about it. I told him somebody's got to do this kind of thing."

Hempel suspected that Dahlberg might quit and start his own pillow-speaker business, so he beat him to the punch and fired him. Dahlberg had worked for Telex for three years. "I had pleaded with him, and I was absolutely sure it would work. But he told me to just do what I was supposed to be doing. But I didn't want to just do what somebody else told me to do…"

Family portrait: Nancy, BJ, Jeff, Ken and Dede, circa 1958. Nancy graduated from the University of Denver in comparative religions and is a freelance writer living in Florida. Dede was a national competitor in amateur figure skating and is an accomplished horsewoman. She has two children and lives in Edina, Minnesota. Jeff joined his father in business and has five children.

The parting was not smooth. "He had promised me five percent of the profits of the company. I didn't know about things like stock and ownership and equity, but I did understand what profit was. I knew the percentage sounded pretty good in addition to my salary. But I never had the wisdom to get this in writing. I had just come out of the Army. You didn't have agreements. Your word was your bond. It was better than that. Your word was so much better than anything written."

Dahlberg had formed a relationship with the controller of Telex, and, as he prepared to leave, asked for his five percent. He was referred to Hempel, who told Dahlberg to take a hike. Dahlberg decided to hire an attorney, and not just any attorney. He hired the lawyer who had just represented Hempel's wife in a messy divorce settlement. It turned out that one of the material items Hempel had managed to retain from the

Marcella Dahlberg, Ken and Arnie's sister and top salesperson.

divorce settlement was a new Lincoln convertible. Hempel offered the car to settle the lawsuit, and Dahlberg was happy to get it.

The change in jobs was not a slam dunk with Dahlberg's wife, BJ. "She cried because we had left this secure job, we had a baby, and now we didn't know what tomorrow would bring. We decided that when we got our business going, my salary would be forty dollars a week. We had to have our groceries."

Dahlberg still had about a thousand dollars of back pay saved up from when he had been a POW. The army continued to pay him $250 a month while he was a prisoner. That wasn't quite enough, though, to get his company going.

"I went to Midland Bank and I got in to see the president, Bob Stebbins. He asked me what I wanted, and I told him I wanted to start a company and I needed some money. He said, 'Well, you need two things to start a business. You need a good lawyer and a good banker.' And I said, 'Mr. Stebbins, that's why I'm here.'"

The banker was willing to loan Dahlberg the money, using Dahlberg's new Lincoln Continental for collateral. The loan was for $2,000, meaning that the total capitalization of the new company was about $3,000.

With his brother Arnie as his business partner, Ken began the Dahlberg Sales Company in Arnie's fraternity house at the University of Minnesota. "We didn't start out with the idea of starting a company, but there was a product, and since Telex didn't want to do it, we decided to do it ourselves. Our first articles of incorporation listed our address as the Phi Gamma Delta House."

Dahlberg began collaborating with Setchell Carlson Radio in New Brighton, an established radio manufacturer. "We took their stock radio, and got a mechanism with a timer on it. The engineers then took the speaker out of radio and substituted this timing device. Then they took the speaker and put it on an extension wire, and the sound came out from under the pillow instead of the ambient air. For a dime, the patient could get their own, private radio listening."

Two engineers were hired away from Telex to do the electrical and the mechanical blueprints on the pillow speaker. Since Dahlberg had no money, each of the engineers was promised five percent of the action and had been given a pep talk by Dahlberg. "Your vision has to be in Technicolor, it can't be black and white. And it has to be in high definition." Eventually both were bought out, having done very well with the Dahlberg Sales Company.

Still, there were big problems to be overcome. "So how do you make a product that is very desirable for the user, but there is no way to pay for it? We wanted to clamp this radio to the headboard, and then you'd put a dime in it and it would play for an hour, and the speaker was under the pillow. Who was going to pay for it? The hospitals loved the idea, but they didn't have any money, either. In those days there wasn't a lot of cash flashing around like there is these days. I came up with an idea that could make money for everybody."

One of the models of the Pillow Speaker Radio that Dahlberg Electronics created.

The idea was fairly simple, but it had one major catch. Dahlberg and the hospital would sign a contract for a certain number of radios, say a hundred at a hundred-bed hospital. At $75 for each, the contract would call for a third party to make the $7,500 investment. For their investment, the investor would get twenty-five percent of the receipts. It was a great idea, except for finding that elusive third party to come up with the cash.

"We would go to the hospital administrator and ask him if he had some favorite people that he had confidence in to share this plan. For instance, did he have a favorite purveyor? And he would say, well, there's Johnny, who delivers our milk every day. We would get two or three recommendations of people to buy this contract. Then we would go to Johnny and say, 'We have this fabulous thing. You'll not only make money, but you'll keep your milk contract safe.' We tell them that they had been recommended to take on this project for the happiness and welfare of the patients and all concerned."

The benefits of the contract would be carefully explained to the potential investor. For their upfront

money, they would get a five-year contract. "If you buy these one hundred radios, the absolute potential is ten cents an hour at twenty-four hours a day, or $2.40 a day per radio, or $240 a day for all of them — but we make no promises."

The venture also included a convenience factor. A patient's friends could stop in the gift shop at the hospital and buy a dollar's worth of dimes. "We just made it easy."

Over the next decade, more than 40,000 pillow-speaker radios were sold to hospitals across the country. During the early years, the pillow speaker was the main and only profit source for the company. Arnie Dahlberg was key in establishing the pillow speaker line, and Dahlberg's sister Marcella was the primary salesperson for the company.

The Dahlberg Pillow Radio display at the National Catholic Convention in Milwaukee, 1950.

Not long after the pillow speaker concept was being developed, Dahlberg began considering getting into one of Telex's lines of work: hearing aids. Dahlberg's erstwhile employer was hosting an international hearing-aid convention in Minneapolis at about that time. Many of Dahlberg's old friends from Telex were there, and Dahlberg signed them up as his salesmen around the country.

Dahlberg went to a tool-and-die maker in Minneapolis with a set of drawings for the molds and stampings of a hearing-aid product. Dahlberg indicated how much he was willing to pay for the work, and the tool-and-die maker agreed to the figure. He told Dahlberg he would take fifty percent down and fifty percent when he delivered the product.

"I told him, 'No, you don't understand. I don't have any money.' And he said, 'How can you expect to pay me if you don't have any money?' And I said, 'When I sell the product, I'll get some money and then

I'll pay you.' And he said, 'No, you don't understand how this world works.' And I said to him, 'Don't you understand that this is the way the world should work? Of course I'm going to pay you.'"

The tool-and-die maker, Harvey Vogel of Vogel Machine Tool, considered this proposition for a while, then agreed to it. "He told me later that it was the first time he had ever taken an order on a proprietary product without a down payment from a guy who told him he didn't have a penny in his pocket. And, you know what, for the next thirty years he had my business without even bidding. That's the wonderful part of the entrepreneurial capitalistic system. It works at a very small level. You've got to get stuff done. You've got to figure things out without a lot of capital. It comes down to trust."

Dahlberg's company soon had a small office in the Calhoun Beach Club in Minneapolis. "We knocked a hole in the wall that led to an unfinished part of the building, and that's where we manufactured. It wasn't zoned for manufacturing, but we sweet-talked the manager into letting us stay there for a while."

In 1951, Dahlberg moved his company into a converted theater in Golden Valley. The building would remain the major manufacturing center for the company for the next four decades. By the time of the move, Dahlberg Electronics already had 100 employees.

DOBBS FERRY HOSPITAL
ASHFORD AVENUE
DOBBS FERRY, N. Y.

CORNELIUS P. LYNCH
ADMINISTRATOR

TELEPHONE:
DObbs Ferry 3 - 4600

May 13th, 1952

TO WHOM IT MAY CONCERN:

Forty (40) Dahlberg pillow radios were installed in the Dobbs Ferry Hospital in June of 1951.

They have been received very well by our patients and have greatly lessened the former annoying noises of radios tuned up to a loud volume.

The radios have been an added source of income to the hospital and the service to the equipment has been negligible.

Very truly yours,

Cornelius P. Lynch

A Pillow Radio testimonial.

Dahlberg credits the Army with giving him a sense of what was possible. "I was perfectly happy at Telex, but subliminally I knew that there wouldn't be much opportunity there with such a limited vision of where the company could go. The most important thing the military did for me was to introduce me to the world. We're all very provincial until we're not."

Ken was the commander of the 109th Fighter Squadron, shown here during its two-week summer training period in 1948. Ken is the seventh from the left in the front row.

The Minnesota National Guard

Dahlberg's time in the Army also gave him a chance to get into the National Guard in 1946. In the next six years, Dahlberg climbed the ladder until he was the commander of the 109th Fighter Squadron in the Minnesota National Guard. The P-51 was not only his military plane, it was also his business plane on occasion, allowing him to travel the country without having to buy his own plane.

By 1952, it became clear that the Minnesota Air Guard would be federalized to fight in Korea. During this time, Dahlberg had a contract with the Signal Corps, a branch of the Army, making highly classified products.

"In those days, nobody had any money, so if you had a party, it was bring your own bottle. We had a little party, a National Guard party, to celebrate that they were going on active duty. In our little kitchen in New Brighton, there were two generals — one was the adjutant general in charge of the entire National Guard in the state and the other was a general of equal rank from the Signal Corps. These two generals were pouring whiskey from their own bottles.

"My bride, BJ, and I were there in the kitchen, and we overheard the Signal Corps general say to the adjutant general, 'Dahlberg is more important to us making this product for the Signal Corps than he would be for you going to Korea making holes in the sky for you.'

"I had been telling the troops that there were no excuses for getting out now that the country needed us. My own inclination was that I wanted to stay in. With a passion I wanted to stay in. But in the end, I got out because the work I was doing was essential to the Army. It was against my own wishes. It was the end of my beloved military flying career."

A 2001 painting by Don Carlson of Ken flying a Minnesota National Guard P-51.

An early Dahlberg Electronics Christmas party. Arnie is second from the left, Ken fourth.

The hearing-aid business made sense right from the start for Dahlberg. "I was in the communications business. Think about it. The beginning of communications is being able to hear. How can you communicate if you can't hear?"

The new product needed a name. "There were two types of names in the hearing-aid industry in those days. One ended in 'X,' like Telex, Audex, Unex. The other half ended in 'tone,' like Sonatone, Audiotone and so forth. One night we were discussing this, and my wife, BJ, said, 'Why don't you just take the last half of one of the common names and the last half of the other?' We said, 'bingo,' and we named it Tonex. Tonex International Hearing."

That hit too close to home for Dahlberg's former employer, Telex, which began a lawsuit claiming name infringement. Moreover, Telex had a witness in California who was willing to testify that one of Tonex's new salesmen had passed off a Tonex as a Telex. The suit was filed in Pasadena.

Dahlberg was still in the Minnesota National Guard, and was a squadron leader. "The planes didn't get enough usage, and so we'd encourage the pilots anytime they had time off during the week to come and fly. The airplanes needed exercise. We'd tell them to go anyplace, to go cross-country, but just to get time in on the planes. So I followed my own advice and criss-crossed the United States setting up distribution for our hearing aids.

"I didn't have any money to defend the lawsuit. I couldn't even afford to go to California. So I flew my P-51 out to California, and I went to see the judge while I was wearing my flight suit.

"I told him I didn't have any money to defend this, and I asked him for his advice. He said his best advice was to change the name of our product to the name of the company we had started with, Dahlberg. He said, 'I know you're not modest about using your name.' He also said, 'You asked for my advice, and if you take my advice and change your name from Tonex, I'll just dismiss the case.' I told him, 'You've got a deal.'"

With the Tonex name dead, Dahlberg Sales Company wanted a better brand name for hearing aids, and eventually settled on Miracle Ear.

Ken with his first business plane, a Beech Bonanza V35, in 1952.

Chapter Ten

Miracle Ear, The Early Years

Going into business was not an easy task for the Brothers Dahlberg.

The hearing-aid business had been a new world for Dahlberg when he started at Telex. One day he was talking to the company's top salesman and asked how the salesman found prospects for the product. The salesman smiled and said there was one great method for being successful. Dahlberg said he was listening.

"He said, 'Everybody knows somebody with a hearing problem. All you have to do is ask, but with a smile on your face.' All you have to do is ask, and you'll be successful all your life. People have the answers to everything, not just the technical stuff, but the stuff you wonder about. It's the ability to ask, rather than tell. I kept asking questions."

Dahlberg said he would ask people who had a hearing problem how they felt about it, and they would answer that they could hear, they just couldn't understand. The sound seemed loud enough, but the person couldn't distinguish the parts of the sound that made speech intelligible.

"When I started my own business, the first ad I created was: 'If you can hear, but you can't understand, call us.' I hit the hot button with that simple, simple statement.

"My question was: 'Where do you get the loudness?' You get it from the vowels, a, e, i, o, and u. That's eighty percent of the power of speech, but where do you get the perception, the understanding? It's the

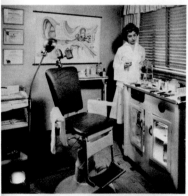
Advertisement for Dahlberg's Hollywood Office.

soft sounds, the consonants. A person might hear an 'a' sound, like in hat, but did the other person say hat or cat or that or sat? We soon discovered that in what we call a cocktail situation, like at a restaurant, in order to understand each other, we raise our voices. But we don't raise the consonants, we only raise the vowels. Even people who have normal hearing have trouble understanding in a noisy place. We decided to make a hearing aid that didn't simply amplify the low frequencies, the vowels, but instead amplified the consonants, the higher frequencies."

After you have an idea, you need capital, and you need to hire the people who will be able to take that idea and make it into a product. Dahlberg would sometimes carve his idea out of balsa wood to give the engineer a concrete example of what he was thinking about. He would go to an electrical engineer to get the components necessary to make the device work. Then he and the engineers would ponder the ergonomics of the creation — how to make it wearable and useable. In the beginning, hearing aids needed two types of batteries, and they were big and heavy. The transistor changed all of that.

"The hearing aid, interestingly enough, was the first consumer product to use a transistor, and it was our company that did it. They used transistors in industrial products before that, but we used it first in hearing aids because we were always looking for smaller and more comfortable hearing aids."

The electrical engineer would identify the components, and the mechanical engineer would determine how to put the components together in the most useful configuration. Then Dahlberg would take these drawings to a tool-and-die maker. "He will make the molds for those toolings and stamp out those parts, the physical components. You're really into a final assembly shop at an early stage. Then you migrate into having your own tool-and-die shop so you can do things quickly and do it the way you want it."

The next step was to buy the components the company couldn't manufacture itself. "The more you could make yourself, however, the better. You can nearly always beat the competition if you can make it yourself."

And that brings up employees. Dahlberg once said in an interview that he began his business thinking that success was ninety percent dependent on the black box, and ten percent on employees. By the time he sold his business, he had adjusted that equation to ninety percent employees and ten percent black box.

Early Miracle Ear display.

"One day in church, the minister said we have a couple from Vietnam, and they need a job, but they can't speak English. He said they were really nice people, and if someone could give them a job, that person would be blessed. Well, I couldn't resist the temptation of being blessed, apparently, so I hired those two people. And I was later to say, when we had about five hundred Vietnamese and Asians working in our plant, what a blessing those two people were. I didn't realize that for the blessing of two, I would receive the blessing of four or five hundred.

"I learned, too, that although I hired them for the dexterity of their fingers to assemble these products, I got their brains for free. And their brains were much more important than their fingers. It was a learning experience for me that was very rewarding. Under the rules of the Employee Stock Ownership Plan, I let the employees buy about twenty-five percent of the company. Some of those who worked the line wound up, when we sold the company, paying off the mortgages on their houses. I had a lot of hugs from that one."

After the bad union experience at Telex, Dahlberg was determined that no union would gain a foothold in

his new enterprise. "They tried to organize us several times, but I had my first loyal gals working on the lines, and they didn't want a union either. It's not that I don't understand the usefulness of unions, and I'm not anti-union from the standpoint of just being an ideologue against the union movement, I'm just against some of the tactics. We were very close in those early days. We had parties and we had picnics — we had a lot of stuff going on. We were a union unto ourselves.

"We didn't need anybody else to tell us how to behave. We paid the employees the maximum the company could afford to pay. My salary was forty dollars a week at the beginning. I was making less than some of the people on the line."

Dahlberg's sister, Marcella, was once called by the IRS to explain why her income was so suspiciously low. (Later when the company was merged with Motorola, Marcella, whose salary was based on sales performance, was making more than the CEO of Motorola.)

In the early days, hearing aids generally came in three pieces. There was a battery pack for two types of batteries; an amplifier, sometimes carried in a shirt pocket, and a speaker in the ear. All of this was connected by wires. It worked, but it wasn't very elegant. Later, the battery pack and the amplifier were combined into one unit, but it was still a bulky and balky proposition.

"I had a concept of what I thought would be the world's first one-piece hearing aid. I carved a model of it out of a piece of balsa wood. I had the idea that if I could get rid of that darn string between the amplifier and the receiver, it would be a better product. That string was the real mark of infirmity in the hearing aid."

The company had a meeting in Denver, and Dahlberg was explaining to his troops in the field about how with the develop-

This page, top to bottom: engineering drafting section; tool and die department; plastic molding/model shop.

Next page, top to bottom: typical parts assembly; test and inspection department; office.

ment of a transistor, to replace the large vacuum tube, the whole unit might be combined into one piece.

"Harold Jones, the dealer from Portland, said if we could make a hearing aid in one piece, it would be a miracle. I said, 'I think you've just named the product.'"

Miracle Ear came into being in 1955.

Dahlberg gives the company's chief engineer, Lester Wilbrecht, credit for the design of the first unit. The aid used three transistors and included a battery, receiver, microphone and various other circuitry parts. All the parts together could be fitted into a unit that would fill a teaspoon. The new product didn't look like the hearing aid seen today, but it was getting there.

The company began marketing three variations of the Miracle Ear. One that fit in the ear, and could be disguised as an earring, was popular with women. One that fit behind the ear was popular with men, and one that fit into eyeglass frames, Optic Ear, was popular with both.

Marketing for the new product was aggressive, using most of the large-circulation national magazines of the day. In 1957, Miracle Ear earned the Good Housekeeping Seal of Approval, a major boost for the product.

The company also pioneered a kit for its salespersons that included an audiometer for testing a person's hearing, and all the equipment necessary to demonstrate fittings and to make ear impressions. The whole kit fit into a briefcase and made the Miracle Ear salespeople both professional and mobile.

The company's original product, the Pillow Speaker Radio, was still selling well through the 1950s, but Dahlberg's company saw a new product come over the horizon. "People weren't satisfied with just radio anymore, because there's this new phenomenon called television, and you've got to have television in the hospital."

The problem with television, though, was the same problem the hospitals had with radio. You can't have every patient with

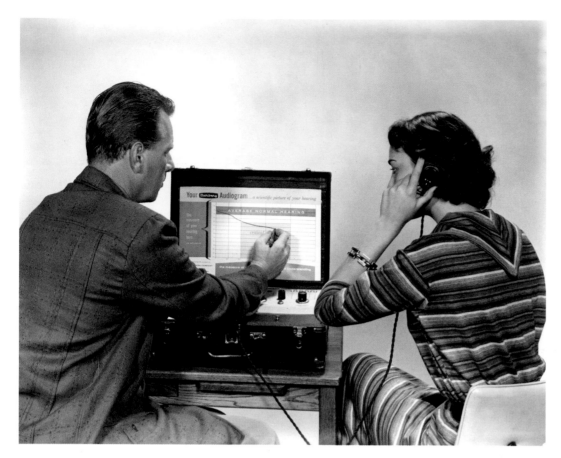
The Dahlberg Audiogram

his or her own television blaring away, disturbing other patients. The need was to create a remote speaker for the television that would be right on the patient's bed.

"You had to hang the television on the wall, instead of the bed, but now how do you get reception? We had to put antennas on the roof, and now we're really getting into engineering projects. And we had to sell it to the hospitals. But there was a change in attitude. Television was such a powerful medium, they just had to have it, or nobody would go to that hospital.

"We had to hard-wire from the antennas down to each room. Then we had to do something new. Instead of just having a speaker remote, we had to put the controls — the on/off switch and the channel controls and everything else — in the speaker remote. But it wasn't really remote because it was hard-wired to the television. You had to have the wire for the speaker anyway, so why not put the controls on it?"

In its way, the Dahlberg Sales Company had invented the remote control for television. No one else had done it up to that point. And the day of the dimes was over. The hospital simply put the use of the television on the room bill.

And while the company was at it, it created a wristband that patients could wear that would be connected electronically to a monitor at the nurses' stations. The wristband would relay basic vital signs, like pulse and temperature, to the nurses' desk. "We didn't know what we were doing, but we were trying to create something that was more desirable."

That development eventually led to more sophisticated communications devices for tying doctors, nurses and patients into one system. "That's what we were doing — hospital communications."

As the years went by, the hearing aids and hospital communications products were all doing well. Among other things, Dahlberg had pushed the development of a pager to alert doctors by combining the technology for a hearing aid with a radio frequency coil, making a walkie-talkie out of it.

"I was at a Young Presidents Organization meeting in Chicago when I met Bob Galvin, who was president of Motorola. While we were talking, I called my wife, who was somewhere in the building, and Bob said, 'What are you doing?' And I said, 'I'm calling BJ.' And he said, 'How far will that reach?' And I said, 'Oh, I don't know, a couple of blocks anyway.' He took it from me and starting talking with BJ, and then he gave it back to me and said, 'Maybe we should talk.'"

WIN A HEARING AID

How many of the world's smallest hearing aids are inside Queen Victoria's Silver Ear Trumpet?

Using the entry form below enter in the number of Dahlberg 1220 Hearing Aids that you think are in Queen Victoria's Hearing Aid shown in the photograph. For the entry to be valid you must enter in the name and address of the person who will receive the hearing aid should you win the competition.

A Miracle Ear promotion

They did talk. In 1959, eleven years after the Dahlberg Sales Company had been founded, it merged with Motorola. Dahlberg's foothold in the hospital business was a key factor in Motorola's interest.

"When we merged, I think our average earnings were $40,000 or so for the past five years. We sold for $4 million. Just think about it. It was one hundred times our average earnings. I'd have to work a hundred years at this rate to get that amount of profit. I could bring forward one hundred years of current earnings right now if we merged.

"But the big companies have more vision than that. They knew something we didn't know. They knew it wouldn't take a hundred years, because the company was growing at 25 or 40 percent a year. Plus we had technologies and ideas that they didn't have. That's why the fifties and sixties were a time of mergers and acquisitions."

One of the groups Dahlberg was intensely involved in throughout that time was the Young Presidents Organization. The genesis of the YPO was with the young service people who had come out of World War II and started their own businesses. They really had few places to turn to for advice or wisdom.

Dahlberg knew a Minneapolis man, Jack Dow, who owned the Hastings Hotel and an advertising agency. Dow had been in conversation with a man named Ray Hickok, of the Hickok Belt Company in New York, and they talked about all the people who had started businesses after World War II.

"We were in the corner office, and we spent a lot of lonely moments because we didn't have anyone to talk to. We couldn't talk to people in our company about policy-level stuff. We just needed somebody to talk to."

People in other disciplines found ways to do it. Religious leaders met. Political leaders met. Doctors got together. But, as Dahlberg put it, business owners would meet only when they ran into each other at, say, the filling station. Dahlberg, Hickock, Dow and a man named Don Knutson of Knutson Construction Company gathered for a meeting.

"If we could organize, if we could get these guys together, it would be helpful to everyone. I was so busy that I didn't do much about it. I was sort of a tag-along. But these guys really got with it. Jack Dow and Ray Hickock put it together."

Ken appeared on the CBS show "I've Got a Secret" in 1967. His secret was that he was awarded the Distinguished Service Cross 23 years late.

Above: Ken and BJ in front of the CBS Studios in New York City.
Below: Steve Allen and Ken on the set of "I've Got a Secret."

The first meeting was in 1952. By 1956, there were YPO chapters all over the nation, and people gathered to talk business, starting businesses, and capitalism. That year, Dahlberg was the chairman of the Twin Cities chapter. After one meeting, a fellow approached him and said that it had been a great experience, but that it was too bad it couldn't have been held in Moscow, the capital of communism. That was all the incentive Dahlberg needed.

"I said, 'I can do that.' I knew some folks in Washington because of my military stuff, and in a couple of days I was in Washington. I said,

The Dahlberg Hearing Aids promotional small car.

'Could we have a meeting in Moscow?' They said that the United States didn't have diplomatic relations with the Soviet Union, but they had just started up a new thing called Intourist where they welcomed tourist groups. I said, 'Bingo, we'll go.' I got a dozen guys, and that was the first foreign meeting of a YPO chapter. Now there are chapters all over the world, and they have meetings all over the world, but that was the first."

Members of the travel group saw the first commercial jet airliner in the world, and it wasn't a Boeing, it was Russian-made. They also met with a young professor of geopolitics from the University of Moscow. The teacher warned them that the United States system had a built-in flaw of trying to give more entitlements to people than it could afford.

"He said the Achilles' heel of our system is that you can't give away more for producing less. He said that history teaches us that. The Roman Empire tried to give away more than they had. So we came away appreciating our own system, but we also had a heads-up that we might have our head in the sand about the notion that we can continuously give more for producing less."

The Young Presidents Organization lived up to its name, and established a rule that when you turned fifty, you were out of the group. Some YPOers graduate to an organization for older executives called the CEO. Asked the difference between the two groups, Dahlberg said, "We do exactly the same things, but it takes us longer to do them."

Dahlberg worked his way up to national vice president, but he had little ambition to go higher. He was mainly involved for that original purpose, to have a sounding board with other people in his situation. He still attends annual CEO meetings.

YPO, and later CEO, were Dahlberg's most important educational resources and became an major part of the couple's social life, providing fast friends and great travel experiences.

Ken and Denis Baudoin were partners for many years in a fishing boat, "Bolo" (below). Ken often used it to entertain Miracle Ear franchisees (above).

Architect's rendering of The Dahlberg Company building in Golden Valley, Minnesota.

Chapter Eleven

The New Era

The years as part of Motorola were years of growth and technological advancement. The hearing-aid division, with Ken Dahlberg in charge, operated much as before the merger and as a stand-alone unit in Golden Valley.

The company's researchers never stopped trying to improve the Miracle Ear family of products. The Miracle Ear IV used the first integrated circuits in the country, and the Miracle Ear V, introduced in 1963, was the first all-in-the-ear hearing aid. By that time, the company had nearly three hundred people working at its Golden Valley plant. The building had been expanded by 23,000 square feet in 1959.

The marriage between the Dahlbergs and Motorola was working well, but in 1964, five years after the merger, Motorola decided to divest itself of all consumer products, including television, radio and hearing aids.

"They were big into chips and silicon, and they were making this stuff for big customers like the auto industry. They just wanted to get out of the consumer business, and Bob Galvin told me I could buy back that division. They had integrated the communications products with their communications division in Chicago, but they had never integrated the hearing-aid division. That made it easy to split the hearing-aid division from the rest. During those five years, I had been running the hearing-aid division, and my kid brother Arnie was running the communications division."

Dahlberg bought the hearing-aid division back for a million dollars. "I went down to the First National

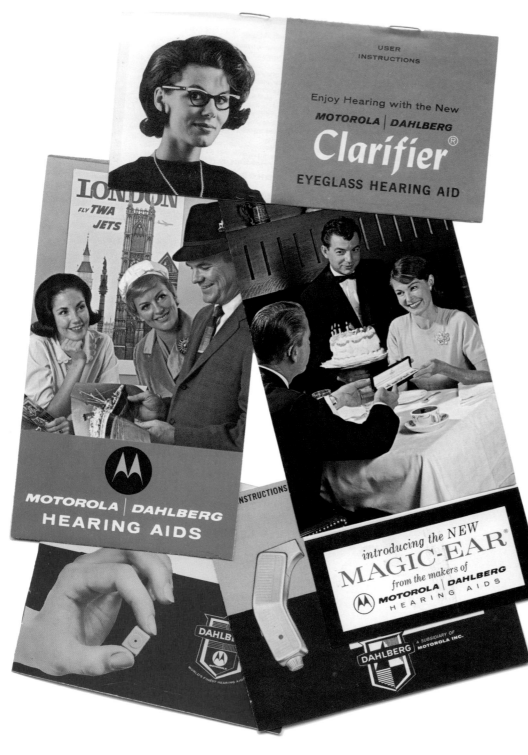

Marketing pieces for various models.

Bank, and I said I want a million-dollar loan. And the loan officer wanted to know what I had for security. I said I've got the security of the company I'm buying. He said, 'That won't do. What else have you got?' I said, 'Well, I've got 20,000 shares of Motorola.'"

When the Dahlberg Sales Company had been merged with Motorola, the Dahlberg brothers had taken a total of 40,000 shares of stock averaging about $100 a share. They had been paid $4 million for their company. The stock later split, and Dahlberg figured out that if they had held the Motorola stock and sold at the highest point, it would have been worth more than one billion dollars. "If we'd just had faith in that stock and not been adventurous…"

The five-year sojourn with Motorola had been good for both sides. "Everybody was a winner. The merger put Motorola into the communications world. Before that, they were heavily involved in the military and made field telephones for the Army. Those were huge things, three or four pounds. What we brought to Motorola was miniaturization. We embedded that technology into that company, and they were ready for the civilian market. They had a head start on everyone. Nokia should never have been born."

In 1964 the repurchased company, Dahlberg Electronics, could focus strictly on developing the hearing-aid business, and Dahlberg turned his full attention to the challenge. The company by then had a sales force of 800 people working in 250 offices around the country.

At the time, the hearing business was extremely territorial. A company like Miracle Ear would sell a territory to a dealer, and the dealer would agree to sell only that line of products. The configuration of the industry soon ran into trouble.

Dahlberg Electronics brochure.

"The Gray Panthers — they were the forerunner of the AARP, if you will — were screaming their heads off that hearing aids were overpriced. So the Federal Trade Commission stuck its nose into it and came down on the whole hearing-aid industry. After they had a whole bunch of congressional hearings, they decided we were price-fixing. They said the whole industry was price-fixing because of these exclusive dealer contracts. They had a law passed that the exclusive contracts were illegal."

The industry argued that the dealership arrangements were not a device to hold up prices and were no different than arrangements in other industries. For instance, you can't buy a Ford at a General Motors dealership. The arguments had no effect on the FTC.

The upshot was that the hearing-aid industry went from about ten manufacturers to about forty in a short time.

The long battle with the government also drained the industry of its competitive resources. When the battle began, the U.S. industry had a hundred percent of the domestic market and seventy percent of the foreign market. By the time the court battles were settled, the American manufacturers had lost all of the overseas market and forty percent of the domestic market.

Dahlberg came within an eyelash of getting out of the business completely in 1969. He was offered a post

On either side of Ken are his European distributors. On the right is Paul Bommer, founder of Bommer AG, later acquired by Dahlberg Electronics.

as deputy undersecretary of defense by the Nixon administration. Hewlett Packard's David Packard was the secretary of defense.

There was just one catch. Dahlberg, because his company did some defense contracts, would have to sell everything and put it into a trust. He would also have to be confirmed by the U.S. Senate. On March 18, 1969, headlines in the Minneapolis and St. Paul newspapers announced that Fabri-Tek, an Edina computer component manufacturer, had acquired Dahlberg Electronics. No terms were disclosed.

In the following days, though, Dahlberg had a change of heart about abandoning the business into which he had put 22 years of his life. The Fabri-Tek deal went away, and Dahlberg went on making hearing aids.

In 1971, the company introduced the Sharp Circuit, which dramatically increased battery life for the Miracle Ear products. But by 1972, with the FTC still hammering away at the industry, Dahlberg again was ready to get into another business. "It's like the company came to a grinding halt in 1972. The focus of the company was to get out of the hearing-aid business. Everybody was tired of the FTC hearings. Even Ken Dahlberg had pretty much given up."

The company began looking into the other parts of its business, particularly into the medical technology field — which had been the original Dahlberg Sales Company's first foray into the business world.

One of its products was called the Correlator. Dahlberg had a friend, Dick Guard, who was an anesthesiologist at North Memorial Hospital in Minneapolis, and one day Dahlberg asked him, "How could someone just have a very healthy EKG, and then die of a heart attack on the way to the parking lot?"

Guard replied that one thing that happens to a body, in the case of internal bleeding or if it is going into shock, is that less blood is sent to the more distant regions from the heart, and more blood is sent to the body core and the brain. If a device could measure the color of the red corpuscles in the micro circulation of the body in the extremities, it could tell if the body was drawing its blood into the central core. The color of the blood would show its oxygen content.

"But what was normal? We took tests of several hundred kids between eighteen and twenty years old, and we got a 'normal.' But now we had to get this authenticated, so we brought it over to the University of Minnesota. We hooked an EKG up to a dog, and then we hooked up our Correlator. The reason we called it a Correlator is that it would correlate the readings from the EKG and the readings from the micro circulation."

The dog tests went well, and it appeared the device was a success — from a technological, medical point of view. There was just one problem.

"I had gotten so deep into the medical, I was so fascinated by the technology, that I forgot something. I didn't figure out who was going to pay for it. Somebody has to pay for it. In this case, it would have to be third-party pay. And the doctors simply would not give that test. We had what we thought were pretty good patents, but at some point you give up. The product was never marketed.

"And now the first thing they do when you go to the hospital is put that probe on your finger. The whole time you're in the hospital, you've got that clip on your finger, and they're measuring your

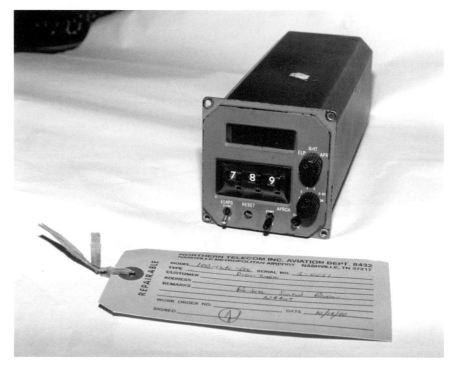

Ken and sales manager Bob Carlson with the first digital instrument for airplanes, the Digi-Timer.

oxygen through infrared. I should have had the firepower to get that product through, but I didn't have enough help around me to get it done, among the other things we were doing. It was a fun experience, and we were almost rich."

The company was also reaching out into other areas. Miracle Ear had as employees two brothers, Don

Civil Aviation

Ken Dahlberg often said that his ability to get around the country in an airplane allowed him to build his company through the years. His first forays into business air travel were actually aboard military P-51s when he was a squadron leader in the Minnesota National Guard. Dahlberg encouraged the pilots in his squadron to fly the Mustangs as much as possible to keep their skills at the highest level. He took his own advice as he expanded his business in the late 1940s and early '50s.

After leaving the Guard, Dahlberg's first civilian aircraft was a Beechcraft Bonanza. It was followed, as the years went by, with a twin-engine Cessna 310 and the first Beechcraft King Air turbo twin sold in the United States. Dahlberg got the plane, which he shared with an FBO in Rochester which used it as a demo, directly from Olive Beech, the owner of the company.

Dahlberg then purchased a Piper Cheyenne twin turbo. He later sold it to a man in England who said he would buy it only if Dahlberg would deliver it to his local airport. To his surprise, Dahlberg agreed. The flight from Flying Cloud Airport in the Twin Cities to the United Kingdom was a little dodgy. Dahlberg brought a friend along for company, and explained to his friend that they could save weight in the plane by not bringing a lifeboat. "You can't survive more than a few minutes in the North Atlantic anyway," he explained. There was some difficulty finding Greenland on the way over, but Dahlberg did deliver the Cheyenne and his nervous copilot to England.

Top: Ken with the Beech Bonanza V35.

Middle: Cessna 310.

Bottom: Lenny Dolny and Ken and Arnie Dahlberg with the Piper Cheyenne.

Dahlberg went without an airplane for a time, but then purchased a Cessna CJ in the mid-1990s, after he sold his company to Bausch and Lomb. Dahlberg now owns a Cessna CJ-2. The airplane has a full-time pilot, Bill Mavencamp, but Dahlberg often takes a turn from the right-hand seat.

The era of aviation is about 100 years long, and Dahlberg has been flying for about two thirds of that time. Here is a short list of airplanes he flew.

TRAINERS

Ryan PT-22 Recruit
Vultee BT-13 Valiant
North American T-6 Texan

FIGHTERS

Curtiss P-40 Warhawk
North American P-51 Mustang
Republic P-47 Thunderbolt

CIVILIAN

Beechcraft Bonanza
Cessna 310
Beechcraft King Air
Piper Cheyenne
Cessna CJ
Cessna CJ2

Top: Ken purchasing the first King Air ever sold from Olive Beech, seated to his right.

Bottom: The CJ2 with Paul Waldon, grandson Carl Hensel, daughter Dede, Ken, Arnie, captain Bill Mavencamp.

A Better Homes and Gardens ad using the tagline, "If you hear, but don't always understand... ."

and Bob Carlson, who were fighter pilots like Dahlberg. In the course of their discussions about airplane instrumentation, the company developed digital controls and readouts. Some of those devices are still standard in the aviation industry. Dahlberg had what he thought was an airtight patent on the digital timer, but so many companies copied the idea that the patent became meaningless.

"We came up with this great idea for a timer. We called it the Digi-Timer, and we sold it to Republic Airlines and other airlines. Out of that same group, we came up with speed control, digital speed control. The new business didn't fit into the hearing-aid division very well, and so a new division was created called Diginautics."

The overall company at this time was still called Dahlberg Electronics, and the company leaders began considering going public. Dahlberg pondered an overall name for the various products and saw that they were all detecting something, whether it was speed or time or hearing, so he came up with Detection Sciences. That was the official name when the company went public. In time, it was changed back to Dahlberg Electronics.

"Everybody was going public in those days. It was just something you did. I was not in that Silicon Valley greed mode. I had my little airplane. I had my house. I was happy. But the company was always tight on money because we were always running on the edge."

Dahlberg was also interested at this time in what in the business world was called "pure play" companies, ones that do one thing and do it well. These companies were more attractive to investors than were the conglomerates that were dominant at the time. Dahlberg Electronics sold a robotics company it had developed. It also sold the digital business to a British company. The lawyer representing the British firm was a Minneapolis attorney named Warren Mack, whom Dahlberg later hired as his own attorney.

The 1980s started as a disaster for Dahlberg's company. With the national economy faltering, the company lost over half a million dollars in 1981. It became profitable again the next year, but the stock continued to hover at record lows. Part of the solution was to once again take a leadership role in hearing-aid technology. The company established an in-house laboratory for hearing-aid molds. The new product was no longer a one-size-fits-all device, but rather was custom-made for the user's ear. Within a few years, the custom-made models comprised half of the hearing-aid industry's sales.

The first Miracle Ear retail store, in the Yorktown Mall, Edina, Minnesota.

At that time, most hearing aids were sold in the home, and a dealer might have a small office in a medical building. But people just didn't come in and buy hearing aids at a business. It was a specialty-selling procedure.

"Our idea was that we could change this industry dramatically, because this was the time when big shopping centers were blossoming. We said, let's bring this industry out of the doldrums, and instead of having an office hidden away someplace, and having a bunch of salespeople going out and selling them in a kitchen, let's make a business out of this. My son, Jeff, gets a lot of credit for this. He was on the front end of it. He was working in the marketing department, and we had hired a franchise consulting firm out of Los Angeles. We developed a concept store. We said we were going to bring this industry into the bright sunshine of public visibility, and we're going to be proud of it. People will come in and buy, rather than having us go out to them. It will reduce the cost to the consumer."

A problem was with the public perception of the hearing aid itself. "A hearing aid was a mark of infirmity. Oddly enough, glasses were a mark of intelligence. Guys like my friend Barry Goldwater would put on great, big horned rims to accentuate the fact that he was wearing glasses. It was a mark of intelligence. I said that we've got to make the hearing aid a mark of intelligence, a mark of caring, that is to say, you care that you can hear your loved ones. If somebody says, 'I love you,' you want to be able to hear it."

Miracle Ear created homey, comfortable offices. The fitting rooms had a medical appearance much like a doctor's office — "although we had to be careful we didn't play doctors, because we weren't. We had to be very careful we didn't cross the line. For instance, we couldn't wear white coats, but we could wear blue

coats that were crisply clean. Or we could wear our colors, maroon and gray."

At international conventions in such places as Acapulco, Miracle Ear used a split-screen technique, showing on one screen the tawdry offices of its franchisees, and on the other screen the concept of the big, bright, clean Miracle Ear stores. "We would just keep flip, flip, flipping these images until everybody was screaming, 'That's enough! We've seen enough.' People were afraid that we'd show their office."

At the grand opening of the first Miracle Ear retail store, from left: Tom Rootness, Chuck Yeager, Wally Schirra, Ken, Jeff Dahlberg and Jane Hixson. Yeager was a famous test pilot and the first pilot to break the speed of sound. Schirra was one of America's first astronauts. Both were on the Dahlberg board.

In one dramatic push, the company changed the concept of the hearing aid and how it was to be sold. "We had to change our own behavior, and we had to go from there into our environment."

The entire industry got a big boost from Ronald Reagan in the early 1980s. First the president helped clear away most of the FTC rulings that had dismantled the industry's franchise organization. Then he appeared in public wearing an in-the-ear hearing aid. Only about twelve percent of people with hearing problems used hearing aids in those days, but the number took a dramatic upswing in the 1980s.

The high-quality product and new franchising arrangement pushed Dahlberg Electronics and Miracle Ear to the preeminent position in the industry. In 1983, Jeff Dahlberg took over as president of the company, and Ken Dahlberg became chairman of the board. The first prototype store was opened at the Yorktown Mall in Edina, Minnesota, in 1984. In attendance were board members, including renowned test pilot Chuck Yeager, and Wally Schirra, one of the original astronauts. Both were part of a national advertising campaign stressing that Miracle Ear used space-age technology. The change in the marketing process was tumultuous, but by June 1984, there were forty franchisees from coast to coast. By the end of the year, there were more than 100.

In 1985, the company spent more than $6 million on advertising, or about twenty percent of its revenues. The goal was to make Miracle Ear a generic term for hearing aids.

Also, during this time, Dahlberg formed a new relationship with Sears. Miracle Ear and Sears had been working together since 1955, but Dahlberg had something bigger in mind. "Maybe it was because the Sears Catalog had been our favorite shopping store when I was growing up. When the catalog became obsolete, it got used in the usual fashion in the outhouse. It was the days before strategic partners, but I must have had some kind of insight. Sears had been important in our lives, and I was attracted to Sears."

Jeff and Ken Dahlberg.

The two sides met at a table, and Dahlberg told Sears officials that if they were going to be in the hearing-aid business, they should get into it in a big way. At that time, Sears was dabbling in the business, buying hearing aids from a small company. Dahlberg pointed out that Sears had hundreds of stores, and was only selling hearing aids in about half a dozen. At first, Sears was not ready to move into the business on the scale Dahlberg had in mind, and bought only a few hearing aids from Miracle Ear to sell in its six stores that offered the devices.

Every electronic product at Sears had a "tone" ending, so Miracle Ear became Silvertone in the stores. In time, the product was in several hundred Sears stores across the country. Dahlberg Electronics was growing substantially.

"And another thing was growing, too — that was the animosity of the franchisees who were competing. We might have a good franchisee, say in Denver, and now you open a Sears store across the street. It was a different brand, but the culture of our company was based on decency and trust, and I knew we had a problem. The only way I could solve that problem was to get Sears to transfer that franchise in Denver to our franchisee there. They said it wouldn't work, because that's a competitor. I told them that I was a competitor now, and that they needed to trust us that we know what's best. It's the power of Miracle Ear that's helping power Silvertone."

Sears eventually came around to the idea, and if the Miracle Ear franchisee met certain financial requirements, he could also get the Sears franchise. Some of the franchisees became huge, owning more than a hundred Miracle Ear and Sears outlets.

The company's revenue rose from $12 million at the beginning of the decade to $75 million by 1990. Jeff Dahlberg left to work with another franchising company in 1986, but returned in 1988. The

The Dahlberg Building in Golden Valley, Minnesota.

franchise concept took several years to become profitable, but by the early 1990s, business was very good. The company began retailing not only through Sears, but also with Montgomery Ward and in Wal-Mart's new superstores.

In early 1990, Dahlberg announced the purchase of a site on Highway 55 in Golden Valley. The company had been running short of space. "I started to do a little reading in those days, like Fortune and Barron's and Forbes, and so I knew I had a little leverage with the village of Golden Valley. So we bought some land in Golden Valley, and the city paid for our move. They wanted us to stay. We built a nice building right off Highway 55, and now it's known as Dahlberg Drive. It's right at the edge of Theodore Wirth Park."

The new combined headquarters and manufacturing plant was a four-story building with more than 86,000 square feet. It included a revolutionary factory-within-a-factory concept that allowed the manufacturing process to be closely aligned with marketing and sales. By this time, the number of full-time centers had increased to 652, with 1,362 service centers and 1,250 sales consultants. The company's overseas sales also were growing. In fact, its position in the industry became so attractive that some of the major international companies came calling.

"It came to pass that our company was more valuable to Bausch & Lomb than it was to us. I had given twenty-five percent of the company to the employees, and so my share was down to about forty percent or so. Our stock was selling for about fifteen dollars a share, and we made a deal to sell it to Bausch & Lomb for twenty-four dollars a share. Then, in their due diligence, they came up with a recent letter from the FTC. I told them not to go there. I told them not to use that letter, but they saw a chance to get their offer down from $24 a share to $21 a share. Sure enough, the FTC pursued it after the sale, just as I said they would. Interesting."

The company Dahlberg had started for $3,000 in 1948 and repurchased for $1 million in 1964 was sold for $139 million in 1993. Bausch & Lomb sold the company again, this time to an Italian company called Ampliphon. "They are a well-run company, and are a credit to the industry and a credit to the community. They do a nice job, and I'm pleased."

To Kenny Dahlberg
With appreciation and best wishes.

A signed photograph from Richard M. Nixon.

Chapter Twelve

Politics

In the 1960s, Ken Dahlberg was drawn into politics. In the turbulent years of the 1970s, his involvement embroiled him in the headline-making events of the time.

"I was totally apolitical. I had not involved myself in politics. I did not come from a political family." But then one day the phone rang.

Barry Goldwater and Dahlberg had remained friends since their days during the war. When Goldwater was preparing his run for the presidency in 1963, he appointed Dan Gainey of Minnesota as his finance chairman. Gainey had been involved in land speculation in Arizona, and had purchased 10,000 acres of desert that later became Scottsdale. He had made his original fortune through Josten's, a manufacturer and seller of class rings.

With the presidential bid looming, Goldwater asked Gainey if he could get Dahlberg involved. Gainey said he didn't know Dahlberg, but he made the phone call, and Dahlberg said yes.

"Dan invited me for a meal at the Minikahda Club in Minneapolis, and in the midst of this meal, he said, 'Now I'll show you how we raise money at the top level. Let me see your checkbook.' I got my checkbook out, and he said, 'Now you will write a check for Goldwater for President. Let's just put a number down, say $5,000.' In those days, that was like putting a million dollars down, but I was just going through this fun game with Dan, and so I did it. 'And, now,' he said very graciously, 'sign it.' I signed it, and he said, 'Now let me see your checkbook.' I gave it to him, and he tore the check out, folded it, and put it in his pocket. He said, 'Thank you for your contribution to the Goldwater campaign.' I told him I could stop payment on the check, and he said, 'I know you could, but I know you won't.' I think that was the first contribution I ever made to a candidate in my life. I didn't even know if I had enough money in the account."

"I became Dan's deputy. He had the first Lear jet, not only in Minnesota, but one of the first in the country. We ran around the country talking to the big shots. I had some marketing ideas for raising money. I had come out of the Neverland of politics, and now I had an epiphany. I got into the Bill Buckley crowd of reading and thinking, and I wound up at the Cow Palace convention fighting Nelson Rockefeller for the nomination."

Goldwater lost his presidential bid, but Dahlberg's interest and involvement didn't go away. He worked fund-raising for Richard Nixon's successful 1968 campaign, then was deputy national chairman and Midwest campaign chairman for the Committee to Re-Elect the President in 1972.

Dahlberg had a close friend at this time named Dwayne Andreas, a neighbor along Lake Minnetonka. They had met when Andreas had snitched Dahlberg's parking spot. The contested parking space was at the Calhoun Beach Club where Dahlberg Sales had one of its first offices.

"It had a coffee shop, and it came to pass that there was a Cadillac convertible in my corporate parking spot all the time. One day I complained to the management in the lobby that somebody was using my parking spot, and I asked him to do something about it. He told me that I could take care of it myself. He said the guy who owns that car is named Dwayne Andreas, and he's sitting at that counter having a cup of coffee.

"I didn't have a clue who Dwayne Andreas was, and I sidled up to the counter and said my name, identified myself, and told him he was parking in my place. I said that if he didn't mind, I'd rather he didn't use my parking place, because I needed it for my business. He laughed, and he was jovial, and he apologized. We became instant friends. At the time, I had like three employees, and Andreas was already a millionaire."

The two became fast friends, and Dahlberg later sponsored Andreas into the Young Presidents Organization. Andreas had started a company in central Minnesota named Honeymead, which later merged with one of Minnesota's agricultural giants, Archer Daniels Midland, or ADM, the "supermarket to the world." Andreas' best friend was Minnesota's most-notable politician, Hubert H. Humphrey.

Through Andreas, the Dahlbergs also got to know Humphrey and his wife, Muriel, and the three couples shared many dinners at their homes.

"Dwayne would say, 'Okay, no politics during dinner. We'll wait until we're in the drawing room for coffee and dessert, and then you two guys can have at it.' Usually, though, we'd just talk about what happened that day, the normal stuff.

The Distinguished Service Cross

"In 1967," Dahlberg said, "I had an unusual phone call from the Department of Defense. They said they had found something in a desk drawer somewhere in the Pentagon with dust all over it. The envelope says that it was undeliverable at the time. He asked me if I was Ken Dahlberg. I told him I was. He asked me if I had done this and this and this, and I told him I was that Ken Dahlberg."

The mystery document was the Distinguished Service Cross, the nation's second-highest military honor, second only to the Medal of Honor. It had been marked undeliverable because Dahlberg was in the Moosburg prisoner-of-war camp at the time it was awarded.

Hubert Humphrey presenting Ken with the Distinguished Service Cross. In the front, from left, are daughter Nancy, BJ, Vice President Hubert Humphrey and Ken.

That evening, at dinner with the Humphreys and Andreases, Dahlberg told the story and said he was asked if he wanted the medal mailed or presented to him at the Air Force base at the Wold Chamberlain airfield. Dahlberg said he had told the official in Washington he'd have to think about it. "And just like that, Hubert said, 'Can I give it to you?' He was the vice president of the United States. All I could say was that I was honored.

"Hubert never did anything halfway. He said I should invite all my friends, and I should give him a list of those friends. We met in the vice president's office, and he had the secretary of defense there, and the entire Minnesota congressional delegation, and the secretary of the Air Force. Hubert read something, and it was one of the telegrams my mother had received saying I was missing in action. He said, 'I know this guy, and he's never missing in action.' That was the charm of Hubert. He always had something super-nice to say. He could say it better than anybody else, because he really had a kind heart."

Republican Finance Committee. Maurice Stans is to Ken's right.

Andreas was a lifelong Democrat and Humphrey's finance chairman, but wanted to make a $25,000 donation to Nixon's 1972 presidential campaign. It was agreed that the contribution would be made under then-current law, which did not provide for identification of large contributors. On April 7, 1972, the law was going to change to require identification of donors. Dahlberg reminded Andreas to transfer the money before the deadline, as contributors to both parties across the country were racing to do. "Dwayne is a really good citizen," said Dahlberg, "and would never do anything that would violate the law."

On April 5 Andreas called Dahlberg from Miami and said, "I put the money in the lockbox at the Seaview Hotel." It was a condominium hotel where Andreas wintered and the Dahlbergs also had a place. Andreas told Dahlberg he'd put the money in the lockbox addressed to the Committee to Re-elect the President, attention Ken Dahlberg. "I had a home in Boca Raton, and I came down every weekend in the wintertime. For some reason, I didn't fly my own plane, but came by Northwest Airlines. Northwest was late, and by the time I got to the hotel, the vault was closed. I couldn't get in, and that was a Friday night."

The date was April 7.

"I called Dwayne and told him that I couldn't get in. He said, 'Okay, I'll send my whirlybird up to get you in the morning.' We lived about forty miles north. He said that he and I and BJ, my wife, would play golf that day at Indian Creek Country Club. I said okay. When the chopper landed at Indian Creek, Dwayne was there in his golf cart, and he had a little brown bag. I put it in my golf bag and zipped it up."

When Dahlberg got back to Boca Raton, he brought his golf bag inside, and BJ asked him why. He said there was a little cash in it.

In fact, Dahlberg had about $50,000 in cash from several people making last-minute contributions to the Nixon campaign before the deadline. That Monday morning, April 10, Dahlberg went down to his bank and, for safekeeping, converted the cash into cashier's checks, including one for $25,000 for the Andreas contribution. He left for Washington on Monday night.

"On Tuesday we had to bring in all this money, just oodles and oodles of money, millions of dollars donated before this law changed. So there I was disgorging all these checks and cash, and I said to Maurice Stans, the finance chairman, 'This one is very special. This one is from Dwayne. It's a cashier's check in my name, but it's the Andreas money. It was received on April 5th, before the law changed, and I called you and you recorded that.' And he said yes, yes, yes. And instead of putting the check in that big pile of stock certificates and checks and cash, he said, 'I'll put this in my pocket so I won't forget it, because I don't want anything to happen to that one.' Well, somehow he must have had a lapse of memory or an ulterior reason I'm not aware of, because he gave it to Gordon Liddy, who was a high-ranking guy on the Nixon staff. You might remember him. He went to jail."

Dahlberg didn't know what happened to his check, but evidently Liddy gave it to Bernard Barker. Barker was later determined to be the number one burglar in the Watergate break-in. He was a Cuban exile who had become a fanatical Nixon supporter because the Kennedy administration had failed to send promised air cover during the botched Bay of Pigs invasion. Barker took the check to his real-estate business in South Florida and had it cashed.

As Watergate became one of the major stories of the 20th century, the FBI became very interested in Barker's activities. "They see in his bank account in Florida that he recently cashed a check from one Ken Dahlberg for $25,000, so, bingo, they've got the linkage between the break-in and the Committee to Re-elect. There it is."

The press later called it "the smoking gun." It was the only real paper linkage between the Nixon campaign and the break-in. Time went by, and Dahlberg was besieged by reporters trying to find out about the check. Keeping his promise to Andreas, he was silent about the donor. "I told the press, and I told Woodward and Bernstein, that there were two reasons I couldn't tell. One was that the guy could sue the hell out of me because what he had done was lawful. And second, I said I wouldn't violate a trust."

While Dahlberg was in Miami for the 1972 Republican convention, he was subpoenaed by the state's attorney for Dade County.

"The state's attorney, who was a big Democrat stationed in Miami, had me picked up by a big, tough goon in a uniform. They picked me up in a squad car, and they brought me down to this little room, and this goon says, 'Before we leave this room, you will tell me where the money came from.' This guy gave me a talk about torture. He didn't physically torture me, but he tickled my torture button mentally, I can tell you. They had it bracketed down to three possible contributors, and they knew that Dwayne was a good friend of mine."

"They had really done their homework. This had been in the public square for about a year. There was just tons of stuff written about Watergate, and so a lot of the dots had been connected for them. But I would neither confirm nor deny anything."

On the way back to the hotel, his interrogator, Chief Investigator for the States Attorney of Dade County

From the "Smoking Gun" Nixon Tapes

The following is a transcript of the recording of a meeting between President Nixon and H.R. Haldeman in the Oval Office on June 23, 1972, from 10:04 a.m. to 11:39 a.m.

Haldeman: okay -that's fine. Now, on the investigation, you know, the Democratic break-in thing, we're back to the-in the, the problem area because the FBI is not under control, because Gray doesn't exactly know how to control them, and they have, their investigation is now leading into some productive areas, because they've been able to trace the money, not through the money itself, but through the bank, you know, sources - the banker himself. And, and it goes in some directions we don't want it to go. Ah, also there have been some things, like an informant came in off the street to the FBI in Miami, who was a photographer or has a friend who is a photographer who developed some films through this guy, Barker, and the films had pictures of Democratic National Committee letter head documents and things. So I guess, so it's things like that that are gonna, that are filtering in. Mitchell came up with yesterday, and John Dean analyzed very carefully last night and concludes, concurs now with Mitchell's recommendation that the only way to solve this, and we're set up beautifully to do it, ah, in that and that...the only network that paid any attention to it last night was NBC...they did a massive story on the Cuban...

Nixon: That's right.

Haldeman: thing.

Nixon: Right.

Haldeman: That the way to handle this now is for us to have Walters call Pat Gray and just say, "Stay the hell out of this...this is ah, business here we don't want you to go any further on it." That's not an unusual development,...

Nixon: Um huh.

Haldeman: ...and, uh, that would take care of it.

Nixon: What about Pat Gray, ah, you mean he doesn't want to?

Haldeman: Pat does want to. He doesn't know how to, and he doesn't have, he doesn't have any basis for doing it. Given this, he will then have the basis. He'll call Mark Felt in, and the two of them ...and Mark Felt wants to cooperate because...

Nixon: Yeah.

Haldeman: he's ambitious...

Nixon: Yeah.

Haldeman: Ah, he'll call him in and say, "We've got the signal from across the river to, to put the hold on this." And that will fit rather well because the FBI agents who are working the case, at this point, feel that's what it is. This is CIA.

Nixon: But they've traced the money to 'em.

Haldeman: Well they have, they've traced to a name, but they haven't gotten to the guy yet.

Nixon: Would it be somebody here?

Haldeman: Ken Dahlberg.

Nixon: Who the hell is Ken Dahlberg?

Haldeman: He's ah, he gave $25,000 in Minnesota and ah, the check went directly in to this, to this guy Barker.

Nixon: Maybe he's a ...bum.

Nixon: He didn't get this from the committee though, from Stans.

Haldeman: Yeah. It is. It is. It's directly traceable and there's some more through some Texas people in — that went to the Mexican bank which they can also trace to the Mexican bank...they'll get their names today. And pause)

Nixon: Well, I mean, ah, there's no way... I'm just thinking if they don't cooperate, what do they say? They they, they were approached by the Cubans. That's what Dahlberg has to say, the Texans too. Is that the idea?

Haldeman: Well, if they will. But then we're relying on more and more people all the time. That's the problem. And ah, they'll stop if we could, if we take this other step.

Nixon: All right. Fine.

Haldeman: And, and they seem to feel the thing to do is get them to stop?

Nixon: Right, fine.

Haldeman: They say the only way to do that is from White House instructions. And it's got to be to Helms and, ah, what's his name...? Walters.

Nixon: Walters.

Haldeman: And the proposal would be that Ehrlichman (coughs) and I call them in

Nixon: All right, fine.

WHO'S WHO IN THE WATERGATE AFFAIR

The cast of characters in the Watergate affair has come to assume the proportions of a Russian novel's. Here is a guide to some of the key figures:

CHARLES W. COLSON, 40, special counsel to the President, general White House troubleshooter and hatchet man, who recommended fellow Brown alumnus E. Howard Hunt for a $100-a-day job in the White House plugging Administration leaks.

EGIL (BUD) KROGH, 31, Deputy Assistant to the President for Domestic Affairs and chief of the White House leak-plugging "plumbers."

E. HOWARD HUNT, 54, public-relations man, mystery novelist (some 45 titles), CIA operative (1949-1970), mid-level planner of the Bay of Pigs invasion. As a member of the "plumbers" unit, he had an ear on eavesdropping operations on White House staffers, and is believed to have been at the Watergate on the night of the break-in. Variously described as "a very Foreign Service type who . . . knew how to operate" and "the dumbest son-of-a-bitch I ever worked with."

G. GORDON LIDDY, 42, ex-FBI agent, ex-Treasury official (eased out for excessive ardor in fighting gun controls), former colleague of Hunt's in the White House, former counsel to the finance arm of the Committee to Re-elect the President (fired for refusing to answer questions about the Watergate affair).

KENNETH H. DAHLBERG, 54, millionaire hearing-aid manufacturer and chief midwest money-raiser for the Committee to Re-elect. Twenty-five thousand dollars in cash handed to him on a golf course by Humphrey supporter Dwayne Andreas dragged him into the affair.

MANUEL OGARRIO DAGUERRE, 69, Mexico City attorney with American corporate clients. His purported signature appeared on $89,000 worth of southwestern GOP campaign money channeled to Liddy and eventually to Barker.

BERNARD L. BARKER, 55, Cuban-born, Miami-based real-estate developer with a taste for intrigue. In Cuba he worked for the Batista secret police, in Miami he helped channel finances for the Bay of Pigs operation (under the nickname "Macho"). Probably the leader of the Watergate five, he made more than 40 telephone calls to Hunt and CRP offices the months before the raid, received $114,000 in Republican campaign checks —and was arrested with four others at the Watergate on June 17.

JAMES W. McCORD, JR., 53, former FBI agent, nineteen-year security specialist for the CIA and "security coordinator" for the Committee to Re-elect. After leaving the CIA, McCord last year set up his own business, McCord Associates, Inc., whose first and only client was the Republican party—until McCord was arrested at the Watergate.

FRANK STURGIS, 37, ex-Marine soldier of fortune with a string of aliases and a reputation as a braggart. He smuggled guns for Castro's rebels in Cuba, then switched sides and helped train anti-Castro guerrillas in Guatemala. Seven days before he was arrested at the Watergate, according to a clerk in a Miami photography shop, he and Barker brought in some intriguing film that suggested the extent of the espionage against the Democrats.

EUGENIO MARTINEZ, 49, former CIA operative involved in smuggling refugees out of Cuba, now a real-estate man in Barker's employ—and a member of his Watergate task force.

VIRGILIO R. GONZALES, 45, Cuban-born locksmith at Miami's Missing Link Key Shop, where he was unhappy and sought an opportunity for new and more adventurous employment with Barker.

Colson

McCord

Hunt

Barker

Liddy

Gonzales

Newsweek magazine on September 18, 1972, identified Ken as one of the "who's who" of the Watergate story.

Martin Dardis, sat with Dahlberg in the back of the car. Dardis turned to Dahlberg and said, "It was Dwayne Andreas, wasn't it?" "I will neither confirm nor deny," Dahlberg repeated. "I know it was Andreas and you just confirmed it with your body language," Dardis said. Dahlberg asked Dardis if he was going public with his guess. Dardis said he would do so tomorrow. (After Dahlberg returned to his hotel, he reported this news to Nixon, Attorney General John Mitchell and Maurice Stans at the convention. He also called Andreas, who just laughed.)

After that exchange and the three-hour grilling under the bright lights, Dahlberg was not happy with his companion but thought he looked familiar. They quickly discovered they were both in World War II. Dahlberg said he was a fighter pilot in the European theater.

Dardis said he was a tank commander for five years, all the way from North Africa to the Battle of the Bulge. Dahlberg said he'd only met one tank commander and that was in the Battle of the Bulge. Dardis said he'd only met one fighter pilot, and "he was the dumbest son of a bitch I ever met. We had seen this American fighter go down behind the lines, and we knew it had crash-landed. I said to my driver, if you think we can make it, let's go for it. When we got there, the pilot appeared on the wing of his P-47 holding his ribs with one hand and his .45 in the other hand pointed at me. He said he wouldn't take the gun down until I'd answered the code word of the day."

"And," Dahlberg asked in the back of the car, "was the code word 'Who won the 1939 World Series?'"

"You son of a bitch, you are that guy!" Dardis said.

To Dahlberg's surprise, Dardis called his favorite Miami Herald reporter from the police car radio. "He got their lead reporter on the phone and said, 'Do I have a story for you.'" The reporter met the two at the hotel fifteen minutes later. At the interview's end, the reporter asked Dahlberg what he would do if

Martin Dardis

Martin Dardis was the tank commander who rescued Ken Dahlberg when he was shot down in Belgium on December 26, 1944, during the Battle of the Bulge. The two later met during the Watergate investigation, but did not see each other again until Dahlberg and Warren Mack conducted an interview with Dardis at his bedside on March 18, 2006. Dardis died a few weeks later from cancer. As you might expect after sixty-two years, his memory of the rescue is somewhat different from Dahlberg's.

I was twenty-one years old, and I was part of the 4th Armored Division in the Third Army. We fought under Gen. Patton, and he was a hell of a guy. I didn't give a damn what he said or what he did just as long as he did it the way he did it.

The Third Army was trying to relieve the 101st Airborne at Bastogne. We saw the plane go down. My platoon commander, who was a good guy, told me, "I want you to get him out of there. Whatever happens, I want you to get that guy out of that field." I remember it was cold that day, my God, it was cold. And there was snow, too.

If we'd taken a tank, it wouldn't have made it. So we took a Jeep, but then we went out on foot. I remember running across a field, and there was Ken, and the Germans were shooting at him from the woods. How he didn't get hit, I'll never know. I was afraid that they'd get a patrol in after him, and then we'd both get nailed. There were Germans all over the place.

He was something else, this guy. He stood up on the wing of this P-47 waving his pistol. He was waving up a storm. As I got closer, he yelled, "Am I in Germany?" I said, "No you're not, you're in Belgium, and we're not Germans." He said, "Who's we?" I looked around, but there were just the two of us.

When we got Ken out of there, the plane blew up.

We got him back to the Jeep, and I told him to lie on his back in the Jeep. The Germans were still shooting at us. The command post was still a long ways off, a hell of a long ways off. The Germans were in the woods, and it started to heat up. We were afraid that when they were shooting at Ken they would attract a lot of attention and they would bring a bunch of people to our position. We thought it would get worse. We got in a tank and got out of there.

After the war, I was working in the state's attorney's office. I went down there to grab him for a subpoena for the state's attorney. Ken never lost his sense of humor in that situation. When they wrote the story in the newspaper, he said, "I should have shot him while I had the chance." I thought that was the damnedest line I ever heard.

But that's how Ken is. He's a damned hero, that's what he is. We were all young kids, but we were tough. Ken was something else. He could have flown that tank if you'd asked him.

You know, I'm trying my damnedest not to cry. I really am. It's not fear or anything like that. It's to think about how long back that was, and how we're all here and we survived. That's the big thing.

THE WHITE HOUSE

WASHINGTON

November 15, 1972

Dear Ken:

As I look back on the election campaign of 1972,
I feel a special debt of gratitude to those who
worked with Maury Stans as members of our
Finance Committee and who, through no fault
of their own, were subjected to some very
rough attacks in the press.

To take this kind of unjustified heat without
flinching is the mark of a big man.

I look forward to the time when I can thank you
personally for all the work you did to help bring
about our victory last Tuesday.

With warm personal regards,

Sincerely,

Days after his 1972 reelection, President Richard M. Nixon wrote a letter to Ken acknowledging the turmoil the Watergate affair had created for those involved.

he had a chance to do anything different. The question probably referred to Watergate, but Dahlberg looked at the man who had been grilling him and said, "Yeah, I should have shot the son of a bitch when I had the chance." The story appeared the next day in the Herald. That quote was its tagline.

Thirty-four years later Dahlberg and Warren Mack visited Martin Dardis, as he lay dying in a hospital in Florida. Dardis explained that it was he who gave the FBI the information linking the White House to the Watergate burglary. It was he who discovered, right after Watergate broke, that the phone calls from the burglars and their defense lawyers were going to Bebe Rebozo, Nixon's best friend, in Key Biscayne, Florida. It was he who went through Barker's bank records and found the $25,000 check with Dahlberg's name on it. And it was he who identified Dahlberg and his importance as a fundraiser for Nixon's campaign. In fact, Dardis claimed that he first offered the story to his favorite reporter at the Miami Herald, who declined to write the story implicating the President. Dardis said his friend always regretted having passed on the Pulitzer Prize-winning story.

Dardis also said he took an instant dislike to Bernstein, who came to his office in Miami looking for the story. But he gave him the story anyway, reluctantly, and was always annoyed that Woodward and Bernstein took so much credit for uncovering the information that he "handed them on a silver platter."

Chapter Thirteen

Carefree Capital

Dahlberg's first foray into venture capital came by accident.

"A friend of mine started a company in the early 1980s called Network Systems. It was a spinoff from Control Data. Well, one time he couldn't make the payroll, and he asked me if I'd loan him $75,000 to make his payroll one time, and I did. It came to pass that he couldn't make the payroll a second time, and so I loaned him another $75,000. There wasn't a piece of paper or anything. This is what you call trust."

Dahlberg was given stock in the fledgling company in return for his $150,000 investment.

"A few years later, another friend of mine, Bobby Piper, asked me to open an account at Piper Jaffray. Network Systems had just gone public, and I had a stock certificate from the company. I brought that certificate into Piper Jaffray and plunked it down on the desk. They told me it was worth between three and four million dollars. I said, 'Holy Toledo!'

"That's what opened my eyes to venture capital. That was the beginning of Carefree Capital."

In 1994 Dahlberg established Carefree Capital to organize his venture capital investments, and hired Paul Waldon to be its new president. The company was named after the city in Arizona where Dahlberg winters. (The name is a noun, not an adjective.) It typically works with six portfolio companies at a time.

Two of the companies it has invested in, Buffalo Wild Wings and The Allant Group, best illustrate the philosophy and approach that have worked for Carefree Capital.

Carefree first started working with Buffalo Wild Wings in 1994 two years after Dahlberg's daughter Dede married Jim Disbrow, the company's lead founder. The former figure skating champion started the company in Ohio and built it into a small chain of restaurants that featured "Buffalo-style" chicken wings and a large assortment of on-tap beer. The company needed an infusion of capital and an experienced board of directors and management. Carefree Capital supplied all three.

With Sally Smith at the helm, the company expanded to 217 locations in 27 states. In 2003 Buffalo Wild Wings went public at $17 a share and by the summer of 2007 had hit $85 a share.

Systemwide, in 2007, Buffalo Wild Wings was approaching 500 stores, had an annual revenue run rate of $1 billion, and employed more than 28,000 people.

For Dahlberg, the magic of this kind of venture capital activity is the thousands of new jobs — both entry-level and higher — that are created every year.

"The impact for me is way beyond what you can get purchasing shares of a Fortune 500 company," Dahlberg said.

Ken's daughter Dede and son-in-law Jim Disbrow. Jim was the lead founder of Buffalo Wild Wings.

The Allant Group is a different kind of animal. Twenty-five years ago with Dahlberg's capital, Illinois entrepreneur Jim Eldridge launched a company that provided mailing and calling lists for direct marketing businesses. The company was profitable and grew steadily without needing new capital for twenty years until federal and state "do-not-call" legislation was enacted.

"We had to recut the company overnight and put a lot of money into it."

Direct marketing firms needed more sophisticated customer information, which could be provided by data-mining and analytics. But this direction was a new one for the company and would require putting together a team of the industry's best and brightest. Carefree provided the capital to cover the losses during this significant transition and offered the expertise to create an innovative culture appropriate for the new direction.

By 2007, Allant's sales had taken off and the industry's Forrester Report ranked it nationally in the top three database marketing service providers.

Carefree's exit strategies with portfolio companies have included both public offerings and private sales. When Dan Haggerty ran Norwest Equity Partners, which partnered with Carefree, he asked when Dahlberg first started thinking about exit strategies. "I guess it was in POW camp," replied Dahlberg.

In September 2007, Dahlberg welcomed his grandson, Carl Hensel, as a full-time employee at Carefree Capital. Hensel is a bright, young business graduate from St. Thomas University who began his career at Buffalo Wild Wings.

Dahlberg's journey from his Midwest agrarian roots through the crucible of World War II to the founding of an international company is a classic retelling of the story of America's greatest generation. Here is how he tells it:

Ken with his grandson, Carl Hensel, visiting the Gué D'aulne estate in 2006.

"The agrarian culture that America started with subliminally supplied the vision and the passion and the energy to create capitalism. The process of knowing that you had to plant, and you had to till the ground, and you had to harvest in order to have something on the dinner table, created the bigger picture of capitalism.

"When we lived on the farm in the 1930s, we had four horses that fed ten people and supplied all the horsepower for a 120-acre farm. That was four horsepower. Now I have a car that has 552 horsepower.

"In those days you had to use that horsepower efficiently. You had to look at the terrain and see how it

The 2007 "Reinvasion"

On June 6, 2007, D-Day plus 63 years, Dahlberg reinvaded Normandy with his grandson Carl Hensel, the authors of this book, Warren Mack and Al Zdon, and friends Mike Dougherty and Paul Waldon. The Normandy visit was part of a weeklong trip Dahlberg made to England and France in search of World War II memories. He was "rising 90," as the British say.

The traveling party at the American Bar at the Stafford Hotel. From left: Warren Mack, Al Zdon, Paul Waldon, Ken, Carl Hensel, Mike Dougherty.

Here are some images of that trip:

❧ On London's Jermyn Street at a "bespoke" shoemaker, Dahlberg explained to the young craftsman that the low-cut aviator's boots that he bought in 1944 were taken by a Nazi guard on a forced march to POW camp in Munich. Could they please be replaced?

That night in the American Bar at the Stafford Hotel, where two photos of Dahlberg and his P-51 hang on the wall along with other World War II memorabilia, we surprised Dahlberg with a copy of the original receipt for the boots from Bunting bespoke shoemakers. The cost: 17 pounds, 15 shillings and six pence. The receipt showed that he put 5 pounds down upon delivery and paid the remainder after he returned bootless from POW camp.

❧ After many twists and turns, directions from a farmer on a tractor lead us to the site of A-2, the steel-planked airfield just above Omaha Beach that was the first landing field used by the Ninth Air Force after the invasion. A large memorial slab marked what had been in the summer of 1944 a hub of frantic activity. Wire mesh from the taxiways was strung on the fence posts marking the now-peaceful farm fields. The low, scudding clouds and blustery wind recalled the D-Day weather that made flying cover so challenging. "This is just like it was in June of 1944," Dahlberg said as he looked out over Omaha Beach.

❧ At Gué d'Aulne, we visited three of the daughters of the estate owners Denis and Madeleine Baudoin. Rosine, who was four at that time, showed us where she ran food from the estate kitchen to the pond where Dahlberg was hiding from the Germans, who were still on the estate. Her sister Sylvie showed us the leather-bound guestbook, which had been sealed upon the death of her grandfather in 1941. An August 1944 entry said that the guestbook had been reopened in honor of the "unexpected visit of a delightful American parachutist." The next entry was Dahlberg's.

❧ With the help of a photograph that Denis Baudoin had taken in August 1944, Dahlberg stood at the precise place that his P-51 of that day, Shillelaugh, had augered into the turf. From there, the photo lined up perfectly with the roof and chimney of Madeleine's sister's house, which, the elderly groundskeeper confirmed, the plane had narrowly missed. We kicked the dirt, hoping to unearth a piece of Shillelaugh, but had no luck. Next time, we agreed, we'll bring a metal detector. Later that day, Dahlberg bid farewell to each of the sisters. "You take care of yourselves," he said as he hugged them, "because I'll be back."

should be plowed to retain the little rain that you got. You had to figure out the efficiencies so that those horses weren't overworked.

"If something wasn't working, you couldn't look in the Yellow Pages and find somebody to fix it. You had to fix it with bailing wire or something. And everything was broken all the time. But the heart of the question was not being afraid to fix it. You had to try.

"The military introduced me to the world, not only geographically but culturally. I saw that it was bigger than my 120 acres. We had been very poor in the Depression, but I witnessed in my travels the very rich all the way to Paris. How did that World War I song go? 'How are you going to keep them down on the farm after they've seen Paree?'

Ken at the American Cemetery above Omaha Beach with daughter Dede on a visit to France in 2004.

"After the war I noticed that with some of my friends, all they had to do was to find a need and fill that need, and bingo, they had a business. That's entrepreneurship. First comes the vision creating the spirit, energizing the passion to execute and then comes the capital. But you had to have a little luck, too.

"Up to this point in civilization, capitalism has proven to be the best system. It has provided more creature comforts and it has solved more of the mysteries of life than any other system.

"Capitalism is based on trust, and too much these days we see a violation of that trust. You can read it in the newspaper everyday. People are tempted to violate that trust because of excess power. It happens when the CEOs of companies get hold of the boards, and serve the dual role of chief executive officer and chairman of the board. In football, it would be like being a referee and quarterback at the same time. It would be as if the president of the United States were also the chief justice of the Supreme Court.

"I have a passion to get this message across. The essence of the free-enterprise system is based on trust, and that trust has been violated. It speaks to our whole civilization.

"The whole thing in the military is that you trust your brother because you know your brother is trusting in you. That's why you do your absolute best, because you know your brother is relying on you.

"It all comes down to trust."

Education and Board Service

Dahlberg loves to quote his teacher in the one-room schoolhouse, who always said, "You'll never learn everything, but that shouldn't stop you from trying." His insatiable curiosity and love for learning led him to spend ten years on the board of Augustana College, four years on the Air Force Academy Board of Visitors, and seventeen years on the board of Hamline University. The Hamline tenure culminated with an honorary doctorate. Presently he serves on the boards of the Phoenix Seminary near his winter home and the Museum of Flight in Seattle, Washington.

In 1970, after Dahlberg declined the post of deputy undersecretary of defense under Richard Nixon, he was approached with another offer. "Instead of taking a full-time job, I took a part-time position on the Board of Regents at the Air Force Academy. They call it the Board of Visitors." Dahlberg was one of four civilians on the board.

While on the university boards, Dahlberg would often purchase textbooks and attend the classes, just out of intellectual curiosity. He credits the university connections with keeping his love of learning and reading alive and well.

BJ has also donated her time and energy to a number of charities. Back in her early days as a homemaker, she was the Republican Chairwoman for New Brighton. In more recent years she has served on the boards of the Courage Center and the Minnesota Landscape Arboretum. She is also a horticulture judge for the Garden Club of America.

Above: Ken receiving an honorary degree from Hamline University.

Below: 1972 U.S. Air Force Board of Visitors. Seated from left: Sen. Howard Cannon, James Reynolds, Rep. John J. Flynt, Jr., Ken Dahlberg, Sen. Ted Stevens. Standing from left: Gordon H Scherer, Lt. Gen. Benjamin Davis (Ret.), Rep. James "Mike" McKevitt, Rev. Frank Haig, Rep. John J. Rhodes, Dr. Glen Dumke, Rep. Charles Wilson.

Ken Dahlberg's 90th birthday began early as he attended the regular meeting of his Christian men's group.

In honor of the July 4th holiday, a few days away, Dahlberg was asked to say a few words about freedom for the group. Not knowing he would be asked to speak, Dahlberg paused a moment and then he began.

"Freedom was the original concept for this nation. It's amazing how Thomas Jefferson and the others came up with those words in the Declaration of Independence: 'life, liberty and the pursuit of happiness.' Jefferson said they were our rights. They are what every American is entitled to. Life and liberty are what we cherish most, what our country stands for. And that marvelous phrase, 'the pursuit of happiness.' What a wonderful way to put it.

"But I tell people that I really don't have to pursue happiness anymore. By the grace of God, I have it."

Ken and BJ at their 60th wedding anniversary, 2007.

My faith has provided guidance for an interesting and long 'first half,'
with a sure promise of an even better and longer 'second half.'
Praise the Lord!

❧ Kenneth H. Dahlberg